Jump Start Your Career
in Technology & IT
in about 100 Pages

Table of Contents

Let's Start !

Acknowledgements

My thanks to all the people who contributed to this book. The Syncfusion team conceived the idea for this book and then made it happen—Hillary Bowling, Graham High, and Tres Watkins. The lead technical editor thoroughly reviewed the book's organization, code quality, and calculation accuracy—Chris Lee. And several of my colleagues at Microsoft acted as technical reviewers and provided many helpful suggestions for improving the book in areas such as overall correctness, coding style, readability, and implementation alternatives—Todd Bello, Kent Button, Michael Byrne, Kevin Chin, Marciano Moreno Diaz Covarrubias, Victor Dzheyranov, Ahmed El Deeb, Roy Jevnisek, Eyal Lantzman, Andre Magni, Michelle Matias, and Alisson Sol.

Chapter 1 Neural Networks

Introduction

An artificial neural network (sometimes abbreviated ANN, or shortened to just "neural network" when the context is clear) is a software system that loosely models biological neurons and synapses. Before explaining exactly how neural networks work, it is useful to understand what types of problems they can solve. The image in **Figure 1-a** represents a typical problem that might be solved using a neural network.

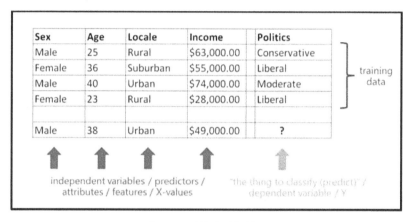

Figure 1-a: A Typical Problem

The goal of the problem is to predict a person's political inclination based on his or her gender, age, home location, and annual income. One hurdle for those new to neural networks is that the vocabulary varies greatly. The variables used to make a prediction can be called independent variables, predictors, attributes, features, or x-values. The variable to predict can be called the dependent variable, the y-value, or several other terms.

The type of problem shown in **Figure 1-a** is called a classification problem because the y-value can take one of three possible class values: conservative, liberal, or moderate. It would be perfectly possible to predict any of the other four variables. For example, the data could be used to predict a person's income based on his or her gender, age, home location, and political inclination. Problems like this, where the y-value is numeric, are often called regression problems.

There are many other related problem scenarios that are similar to the one shown in **Figure 1-a**. For example, you could have several million x-values where each represents the pixel value in a photograph of a person, and a y-value that represents the class of the picture, such as "on security watch list" or "not on watch list". Such problems are sometimes called image recognition problems. Or imagine x-values that represent digitized audio signals and y-values that represent vocabulary words such as "hello" and "quit". This is speech recognition.

Neural networks are not magic and require data with known y-values, called the training data. In **Figure 1-a** there are only four training items. In a realistic scenario you would likely have hundreds or thousands of training items.

The diagram in **Figure 1-b** represents a neural network that predicts the political inclination of a male who is 35 years old, lives in a rural area, and has an annual income of $49,000.00.

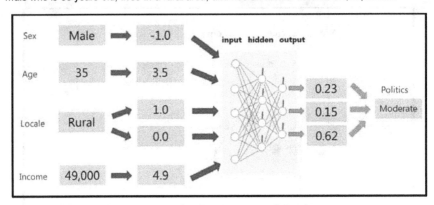

Figure 1-b: A Neural Network

As you will see shortly, a neural network is essentially a complicated mathematical function that understands only numbers. So, the first step when working with a neural network is to encode non-numeric x-data, such as gender and home location, into numeric data. In **Figure 1-b**, "male" is encoded as -1.0 and "rural" is encoded as (1.0, 0.0).

In addition to encoding non-numeric x-data, in many problems numeric x-data is normalized so that the magnitudes of the values are all roughly in the same range. In **Figure 1-b**, the age value of 35 is normalized to 3.5 and the income value of $49,000.00 is normalized to 4.9. The idea is that without normalization, x-variables that have values with very large magnitudes can dominate x-variables that have values with small magnitudes.

The heart of a neural network is represented by the central box. A typical neural network has three levels of nodes. The input nodes hold the x-values. The hidden nodes and output nodes perform processing. In **Figure 1-b**, the output values are (0.23, 0.15, 0.62). These three values loosely represent the probability of conservative, liberal, and moderate respectively. Because the y-value associated with moderate is the highest, the neural network concludes that the 35-year-old male has a political inclination that is moderate.

The dummy neural network in **Figure 1-b** has 5 input nodes, 4 hidden nodes, and 3 output nodes. The number of input and output nodes are determined by the structure of the problem data. But the number of hidden nodes can vary and is typically found through trial and error. Notice the neural network has (5 * 4) + (4 * 3) = 32 lines connecting the nodes. Each of these lines represents a numeric value, for example -1.053 or 3.987, called a weight. Also, each hidden and output node (but not the input nodes) has an additional special kind of weight, shown as a red line in the diagram. These special weights are called biases.

A neural network's output values are determined by the values of the inputs and the values of the weights and biases. So, the real question when using a neural network to make predictions is how to determine the values of the weights and biases. This process is called training.

Put another way, training a neural network involves finding a set of values for the weights and biases so that when presented with training data, the computed outputs closely match the known, desired output values. Once the network has been trained, new data with unknown y-values can be presented and a prediction can be made.

This book will show you how to create neural network systems from scratch using the C# programming language. There are existing neural network applications you can use, so why bother creating your own? There are at least four reasons. First, creating your own neural network gives you complete control over the system and allows you to customize the system to meet specific problems. Second, if you learn how to create a neural network from scratch, you gain a full understanding of how neural networks work, which allows you to use existing neural network applications more effectively. Third, many of the programming techniques you learn when creating neural networks can be used in other programming scenarios. And fourth, you might just find creating neural networks interesting and entertaining.

Data Encoding and Normalization

One of the essential keys to working with neural networks is understanding data encoding and normalization. Take a look at the screenshot of a demo program in **Figure 1-c**. The demo program begins by setting up four hypothetical training data items with x-values for people's gender, age, home location, and annual income, and y-values for political inclination (conservative, liberal, or moderate). The first line of dummy data is:

```
Male  25  Rural   63,000.00  Conservative
```

The demo performs encoding on the non-numeric data (gender, locale, and politics). There are two kinds of encoding used, effects encoding for non-numeric x-values and dummy encoding for non-numeric y-values. The first line of the resulting encoded data is:

```
-1  25  1 0  63,000.00  1 0 0
```

After all data has been converted to numeric values, the data is stored into a matrix in memory and displayed. Next, the demo performs normalization on the numeric x-values (age and income). The first line of encoded and normalized data is:

```
-1.00  -0.84  1.00 0.00  0.76  1.00 0.00 0.00
```

The demo uses two different types of normalization, Gaussian normalization on the age values, and min-max normalization on the income values. Values that are Gaussian normalized take on values that are typically between -10.0 and +10.0. Values that are min-max normalized usually take on values that are between 0.0 and 1.0, or between -1.0 and +1.0.

The demo program uses two different types of normalization just to illustrate the two techniques. In most realistic situations you would use either Gaussian or min-max normalization for a problem, but not both. As a general rule of thumb, min-max normalization is more common than Gaussian normalization.

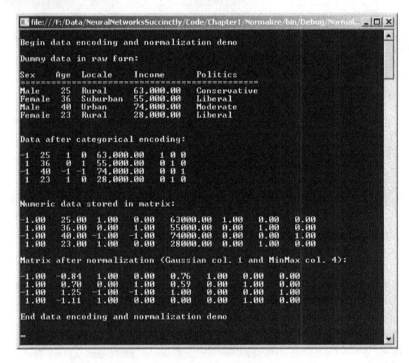

Figure 1-c: Data Encoding and Normalization

Overall Demo Program Structure

To create the demo program, I opened Visual Studio, selected the C# console application project template, and named it Normalize. The demo program has no significant .NET version dependencies, so any version of Visual Studio should work. After the template code loaded in the editor, in the Solution Explorer window I renamed the Program.cs file to the slightly more descriptive NormalizeProgram.cs, and Visual Studio automatically renamed the Program class.

At the top of the source code I deleted all using statements except the one that references the top-level System namespace. The demo was written using a static-method approach rather than an object-oriented approach for simplicity and ease of refactoring.

The overall structure of the demo program is presented in **Listing 1-a**. Methods GaussNormal and MinMaxNormal operate on a matrix of numeric values and normalize a single column of the matrix. Methods ShowMatrix and ShowData are just convenience helpers to keep the Main method a bit tidier. Method EncodeFile operates on a text file and performs either effects encoding or dummy encoding on a specified column of the file.

Methods EffectsEncoding and DummyEncoding are helpers that are called by the method EncodeFile. The demo program has all normal error-checking code removed in order to keep the main ideas as clear as possible.

```
using System;
namespace Normalize
{
  class NormalizeProgram
  {
    static void Main(string[] args)
    {
      Console.WriteLine("\nBegin data encoding and normalization demo\n");

      // Set up raw source data.
      // Encode and display data.
      // Normalize and display data.

      Console.WriteLine("\nEnd data encoding and normalization demo\n");
      Console.ReadLine();
    }

    static void GaussNormal(double[][] data, int column) { . . }

    static void MinMaxNormal(double[][] data, int column) { . . }

    static void ShowMatrix(double[][] matrix, int decimals) { . . }

    static void ShowData(string[] rawData) { . . }

    static void EncodeFile(string originalFile, string encodedFile,
      int column, string encodingType) { . . }

    static string EffectsEncoding(int index, int N) { . . }

    static string DummyEncoding(int index, int N) { . . }

  } // Program class
} // ns
```

Listing 1-a: Encoding and Normalization Demo Program Structure

All program control logic is contained in method Main. The method definition begins:

```
static void Main(string[] args)
{
  Console.WriteLine("\nBegin data encoding and normalization demo\n");
  string[] sourceData = new string[] {
```

```
"Sex     Age Locale   Income      Politics",
"=================================================",
"Male     25  Rural    63,000.00   Conservative",
"Female   36  Suburban 55,000.00   Liberal",
"Male     40  Urban    74,000.00   Moderate",
"Female   23  Rural    28,000.00   Liberal" };
```

Four lines of dummy data are assigned to an array of strings named sourceData. The items in each string are artificially separated by multiple spaces for readability. Next, the demo displays the dummy source data by calling helper method ShowData:

```
Console.WriteLine("Dummy data in raw form:\n");
ShowData(sourceData);
```

The helper display method is defined:

```
static void ShowData(string[] rawData)
{
  for (int i = 0; i < rawData.Length; ++i)
    Console.WriteLine(rawData[i]);
  Console.WriteLine("");
}
```

Next, the demo program manually sets up and displays an encoded version of the dummy source data:

```
string[] encodedData = new string[] {
  "-1  25   1  0  63,000.00   1 0 0",
  " 1  36   0  1  55,000.00   0 1 0",
  "-1  40  -1 -1  74,000.00   0 0 1",
  " 1  23   1  0  28,000.00   0 1 0" };

Console.WriteLine("\nData after categorical encoding:\n");
ShowData(encodedData);
```

Again, the items are artificially separated by multiple spaces. Because there are only four lines of training data, the data was manually encoded. In most situations, training data will be in a text file and will not be manually encoded, but will be encoded in one of two ways. The first approach to encoding training data in a text file is to use the copy and paste feature in a text editor such as Notepad. This is generally feasible with relatively small files (say, fewer than 500 lines) that have relatively few categorical values (about 10 or less).

The second approach is to programmatically encode data in a text file. Exactly how to encode non-numeric data and how to programmatically encode data stored in a text file will be explained shortly.

After all non-numeric data has been encoded to numeric values, the dummy data is manually stored into a matrix and displayed:

```
Console.WriteLine("\nNumeric data stored in matrix:\n");
double[][] numericData = new double[4][];
numericData[0] = new double[] { -1, 25.0,  1,  0, 63000.00, 1, 0, 0 };
numericData[1] = new double[] {  1, 36.0,  0,  1, 55000.00, 0, 1, 0 };
```

```
numericData[2] = new double[] { -1, 40.0, -1, -1, 74000.00, 0, 0, 1 };
numericData[3] = new double[] {  1, 23.0,  1,  0, 28000.00, 0, 1, 0 };
ShowMatrix(numericData, 2);
```

In most situations, your encoded data will be in a text file and programmatically loaded into a matrix along the lines of:

```
double[][] numericData = LoadData("..\\EncodedDataFile");
```

Example code to load a matrix from a text file is presented and fully explained in Chapter 5. Helper method ShowMatrix is defined:

```
static void ShowMatrix(double[][] matrix, int decimals)
{
  for (int i = 0; i < matrix.Length; ++i)
  {
    for (int j = 0; j < matrix[i].Length; ++j)
    {
      double v = Math.Abs(matrix[i][j]);
      if (matrix[i][j] >= 0.0)
        Console.Write(" ");
      else
        Console.Write("-");
      Console.Write(v.ToString("F" + decimals).PadRight(5) + " ");
    }
    Console.WriteLine("");
  }
}
```

Neural network systems make extensive use of matrices. Even if you are an experienced programmer, unless you have done numerical or scientific programming, you may not be very familiar with working with matrices. Here, a matrix is defined as an array of arrays. Unlike many programming languages, C# supports a true multidimensional-array style matrix. For example:

```
double[,] matrix = new double[3,2]; // 3 rows and 2 cols.
```

However, for neural network systems, array-of-arrays style matrices are more convenient to work with because each row can be referenced as a separate array.

The Main method concludes by programmatically normalizing the age and income columns (columns 1 and 4) of the data matrix:

```
  GaussNormal(numericData, 1);
  MinMaxNormal(numericData, 4);

  Console.WriteLine("\nMatrix after normalization (Gaussian col. 1" +
    " and MinMax col. 4):\n");
  ShowMatrix(numericData, 2);

  Console.WriteLine("\nEnd data encoding and normalization demo\n");
  Console.ReadLine();
} // Main
```

In most situations, numeric x-data will be normalized using either Gaussian or min-max but not both. However, there are realistic scenarios where both types of normalization are used on a data set.

Effects Encoding and Dummy Encoding

Encoding non-numeric y-data to numeric values is usually done using a technique called 1-of-N dummy encoding. In the demo, the y-variable to predict can take one of three values: conservative, liberal, or moderate. To encode N non-numeric values, you use N numeric variables like so:

```
conservative -> 1 0 0
liberal      -> 0 1 0
moderate     -> 0 0 1
```

You can think of each of the three values representing the amount of "conservative-ness", "liberal-ness", and "moderate-ness" respectively.

The ordering of the dummy encoding associations is arbitrary, but if you imagine each item has an index (0, 1, and 2 for conservative, liberal, and moderate respectively), notice that item 0 is encoded with a 1 in position 0 and 0s elsewhere; item 1 is encoded with a 1 in position 1 and 0s elsewhere; and item 2 is encoded with a 1 in position 2 and 0s elsewhere. So, in general, item i is encoded with a 1 at position i and 0s elsewhere.

Situations where the dependent y-value to predict can take only one of two possible categorical values, such as "male" or "female", can be considered a special case. You can encode such values using standard dummy encoding:

```
male   -> 1 0
female -> 0 1
```

Alternatively, you can encode using a simple 0-1 encoding like so:

```
male   -> 1
female -> 0
```

An alternative that is not recommended is to encode non-numeric values along the lines of:

```
conservative -> 1
liberal      -> 2
moderate     -> 3
```

A detailed explanation of why this encoding scheme is usually not a good approach is a bit subtle and is outside the scope of this chapter. But, in short, even though such a scheme works, it usually makes it more difficult for a neural network to learn good weights and bias values.

Encoding non-numeric x-data to numeric values can be done in several ways, but using what is called 1-of-(N-1) effects encoding is usually a good approach. The idea is best explained by example. In the demo, the x-variable home locale can take one of three values: rural, suburban, or urban. To encode N non-numeric values you use N-1 numeric variables like this:

```
rural      ->   1   0
suburban   ->   0   1
urban      ->  -1  -1
```

As with dummy encoding, the order of the associations is arbitrary. You might have expected to use 1-of-*N* dummy encoding for x-data. However, for x-data, using 1-of-(*N*-1) effects encoding is usually much better. Again, the underlying math is a bit subtle.

You might also have expected the encoding for the last item, "urban", to be either (0, 0) or (1, 1) instead of (-1, -1). This is in fact possible; however, using all -1 values for effects encoding the last item in a set typically generates a better neural network prediction model.

Encoding independent x-data which can take only one of two possible categorical values, such as "left-handed" or "right-handed", can be considered a special case of effects encoding. In such situations, you should always encode one value as -1 and the other value as +1. The common computer-science approach of using a 0-1 encoding scheme, though seemingly more natural, is definitely inferior and should not be used.

In summary, to encode categorical independent x-data, use 1-of-(*N*-1) effects encoding unless the predictor feature is binary, in which case use a -1 and +1 encoding. To encode categorical y-data, use 1-of-*N* dummy encoding unless the feature to be predicted is binary, in which case you can use either regular 1-of-*N* dummy encoding, or use 0-1 encoding.

Programmatically encoding categorical data is usually done before any other processing occurs. Programmatically encoding a text file is not entirely trivial. To do so, it is useful to define two helper methods. First, consider helper method EffectsEncoding in **Listing 1-b**.

```
static string EffectsEncoding(int index, int N)
{
  if (N == 2)
  {
    if (index == 0) return "-1";
    else if (index == 1) return "1";
  }

  int[] values = new int[N-1];
  if (index == N-1) // Last item is all -1s.
  {
    for (int i = 0; i < values.Length; ++i)
      values[i] = -1;
  }
  else
  {
    values[index] = 1; // 0 values are already there.
  }

  string s = values[0].ToString();
  for (int i = 1; i < values.Length; ++i)
    s += "," + values[i];
  return s;
}
```

Listing 1-b: Helper Method for Effects Encoding

Method EffectsEncoding accepts an index value for a categorical value and the number of possible items the categorical value can take, and returns a string. For example, in the demo program, the x-data locale can take one of three values (rural, suburban, urban). If the input parameters to method EffectsEncoding are 0 (corresponding to rural) and 3 (the number of possible values), then a call to EffectsEncoding (0, 3) returns the string "1,0".

Helper method EffectsEncoding first checks for the special case where the x-data to be encoded can only be one of two possible values. Otherwise, the method creates an integer array corresponding to the result, and then constructs a comma-delimited return string from the array.

Method EffectsEncoding assumes that items are comma-delimited. You may want to pass the delimiting character to the method as an input parameter.

Now consider a second helper method, DummyEncoding, that accepts the index of a dependent y-variable and the total number of categorical values, and returns a string corresponding to dummy encoding. For example, if a y-variable is political inclination with three possible values (conservative, liberal, moderate), then a call to DummyEncoding(2, 3) is a request for the dummy encoding of item 2 (liberal) of 3, and the return string would be "0,0,1".

The DummyEncoding method is defined:

```
static string DummyEncoding(int index, int N)
{
  int[] values = new int[N];
  values[index] = 1;

  string s = values[0].ToString();
  for (int i = 1; i < values.Length; ++i)
    s += "," + values[i];
  return s;
}
```

The DummyEncoding method makes the assumption that items are comma-delimited, and skips normal error checking. The method also uses simple string concatenation rather than the more efficient StringBuilder class. The ability to take such shortcuts that can greatly decrease code size and complexity is an advantage of writing your own neural network code from scratch.

Method EncodeFile accepts a path to a text file (which is assumed to be comma-delimited and without a header line), a 0-based column to encode, and a string that can have the value "effects" or "dummy". The method creates an encoded text file. Note that the demo program uses manual encoding rather than calling method EncodeFile.

Suppose a set of raw training data that corresponds to the demo program in **Figure 1-c** resides in a text file named Politics.txt, and is:

```
Male,25,Rural,63000.00,Conservative
Female,36,Suburban,55000.00,Liberal
Male,40,Urban,74000.00,Moderate
Female,23,Rural,28000.00,Liberal
```

A call to EncodeFile("Politics.txt", "PoliticsEncoded.txt", 2, "effects") would generate a new file named PoliticsEncoded.txt with contents:

```
Male,25,1,0,63000.00,Conservative
Female,36,0,1,55000.00,Liberal
Male,40,-1,-1,74000.00,Moderate
Female,23,1,0,28000.00,Liberal
```

To encode multiple columns, you could call EncodeFile several times or write a wrapper method to do so. In the demo, the definition of method EncodeFile begins:

```
static void EncodeFile(string originalFile, string encodedFile,
  int column, string encodingType)
{
  // encodingType: "effects" or "dummy"
  FileStream ifs = new FileStream(originalFile, FileMode.Open);
  StreamReader sr = new StreamReader(ifs);
  string line = "";
  string[] tokens = null;
```

Instead of the simple but crude approach of passing the encoding type as a string, you might want to consider using an Enumeration type. The code assumes that the namespace System.IO is in scope. Alternatively, you can fully qualify your code. For example, System.IO.FileStream.

Method EncodeFile performs a preliminary scan of the target column in the source text file and creates a dictionary of the distinct items in the column:

```
Dictionary<string, int> d = new Dictionary<string,int>();
int itemNum = 0;
while ((line = sr.ReadLine()) != null)
{
  tokens = line.Split(','); // Assumes items are comma-delimited.
  if (d.ContainsKey(tokens[column]) == false)
    d.Add(tokens[column], itemNum++);
}
sr.Close();
ifs.Close();
```

The code assumes there is no header line in the source file. You might want to pass a Boolean parameter named something like hasHeader, and if true, read and save the first line of the source file. The code also assumes the namespace System.Collections.Generic is in scope, and that the file is comma-delimited. There is always a balance between defining a method that is simple but not very robust or general, and using a significant amount of extra code (often roughly twice as many lines or more) to make the method more robust and general.

For the Dictionary object, the key is a string which is an item in the target column—for example, "urban". The value is a 0-based item number—for example, 2. Method EncodeFile continues by setting up the mechanism to write the result text file:

```
int N = d.Count; // Number of distinct strings.

ifs = new FileStream(originalFile, FileMode.Open);
sr = new StreamReader(ifs);
```

```
FileStream ofs = new FileStream(encodedFile, FileMode.Create);
StreamWriter sw = new StreamWriter(ofs);
string s = null; // Result line.
```

As before, no error checking is performed to keep the main ideas clear. Method EncodeFile traverses the source text file and extracts the strings in the current line:

```
while ((line = sr.ReadLine()) != null)
{
  s = "";
  tokens = line.Split(','); // Break apart strings.
```

The tokens from the current line are scanned. If the current token is not in the target column it is added as-is to the output line, but if the current token is in the target column it is replaced by the appropriate encoding:

```
for (int i = 0; i < tokens.Length; ++i) // Reconstruct.
{
  if (i == column) // Encode this string.
  {
    int index = d[tokens[i]]; // 0, 1, 2, or . . .
    if (encodingType == "effects")
      s += EffectsEncoding(index, N) + ",";
    else if (encodingType == "dummy")
      s += DummyEncoding(index, N) + ",";
  }
  else
    s += tokens[i] +",";
}
```

Method EncodeFile concludes:

```
    s.Remove(s.Length - 1); // Remove trailing ','.
    sw.WriteLine(s); // Write the string to file.
  } // while

  sw.Close(); ofs.Close();
  sr.Close(); ifs.Close();
}
```

The current result line will have a trailing comma (or whatever delimiting character you specify if you parameterize the method), so the very convenient String.Remove method is used to strip the trailing character away before writing the result line.

Min-Max Normalization

Perhaps the best way to explain min-max normalization is by using a concrete example. In the demo, the age data values are 25, 36, 40, and 23. To compute the min-max normalized value of one of a set of values you need the minimum and maximum values of the set. Here min = 23 and max = 40. The min-max normalized value for the first age, 25, is (25 - 23) / (40 - 23) = 2 / 17 = 0.118. In general, the min-max normalized value for some value x is $(x - min) / (max - min)$—very simple.

The definition of method MinMaxNormal begins:

```
static void MinMaxNormal(double[][] data, int column)
{
  int j = column;
  double min = data[0][j];
  double max = data[0][j];
```

The method accepts a numeric matrix and a 0-based column to normalize. Notice the method returns void; it operates directly on its input parameter matrix and modifies it. An alternative would be to define the method so that it returns a matrix result.

Method MinMaxNormal begins by creating a short alias named j for the parameter named column. This is just for convenience. Local variables min and max are initialized to the first available value (the value in the first row) of the target column.

Next, method MinMaxNormal scans the target column and finds the min and max values there:

```
for (int i = 0; i < data.Length; ++i)
{
  if (data[i][j] < min)
    min = data[i][j];
  if (data[i][j] > max)
    max = data[i][j];
}
```

Next, MinMaxNormal performs an error check:

```
double range = max - min;
if (range == 0.0) // ugly
{
  for (int i = 0; i < data.Length; ++i)
    data[i][j] = 0.5;
  return;
}
```

If both min and max have the same value, then all the values in the target column must be the same. Here, the response to that situation is to arbitrarily normalize all values to 0.5. An alternative is to throw an exception or display a warning message. If all the values of some independent predictor variable are the same, then that variable contains no useful information for prediction.

Notice the demo code makes an explicit equality comparison check between two values that are type double. In practice this is not a problem, but a safer approach is to check for closeness. For example:

```
if (Math.Abs(range) < 0.00000001)
```

Method MinMaxNormal concludes by performing the normalization:

```
  for (int i = 0; i < data.Length; ++i)
    data[i][j] = (data[i][j] - min) / range;
}
```

Notice that if the variable range has a value of 0, there would be a divide-by-zero error. However, the earlier error-check eliminates this possibility.

Gaussian Normalization

Gaussian normalization is also called standard score normalization. Gaussian normalization is best explained using an example. The age values in the demo are 25, 36, 40, and 23. The first step is to compute the mean (average) of the values:

mean = (25 + 36 + 40 + 23) / 4 = 124 / 4 = 31.0

The next step is to compute the standard deviation of the values:

stddev = sqrt(($(25 - 31)^2$ + $(36 - 31)^2$ + $(40 - 31)^2$ + $(23 - 31)^2$) / 4)

= sqrt((36 + 25 + 81 + 64) / 4)

= sqrt(206 / 4)

= sqrt(51.5)

= 7.176

In words, "take each value, subtract the mean, and square it. Add all those terms, divide by the number of values, and then take the square root."

The Gaussian normalized value for 25 is (25 - 31.0) / 7.176 = -0.84 as shown in **Figure 1-c**. In general, the Gaussian normalized value for some value x is $(x - mean)$ / stddev.

The definition of method GaussNormal begins:

```
static void GaussNormal(double[][] data, int column)
{
  int j = column; // Convenience.
  double sum = 0.0;
  for (int i = 0; i < data.Length; ++i)
    sum += data[i][j];
  double mean = sum / data.Length;
```

The mean is computed by adding each value in the target column of the data matrix parameter. Notice there is no check to verify that the data matrix is not null. Next, the standard deviation of the values in the target column is computed:

```
double sumSquares = 0.0;
for (int i = 0; i < data.Length; ++i)
  sumSquares += (data[i][j] - mean) * (data[i][j] - mean);
double stdDev = Math.Sqrt(sumSquares / data.Length);
```

Method GaussNormal computes what is called the population standard deviation because the sum of squares term is divided by the number of values in the target column (in term data.Length). An alternative is to use what is called the sample standard deviation by dividing the sum of squares term by one less than the number of values:

```
double stdDev = Math.Sqrt(sumSquares / (data.Length - 1));
```

When performing Gaussian normalization on data for use with neural networks, it does not matter which version of standard deviation you use. Method GaussNormal concludes:

```
  for (int i = 0; i < data.Length; ++i)
    data[i][j] = (data[i][j] - mean) / stdDev;
}
```

A fatal exception will be thrown if the value in variable stdDev is 0, but this cannot happen unless all the values in the target column are equal. You might want to add an error-check for this condition.

Complete Demo Program Source Code

```
using System;
//using System.IO; // for EncodeFile
//using System.Collections.Generic;

// The demo code violates many normal style conventions to keep the size small.

namespace Normalize
{
  class NormalizeProgram
  {
    static void Main(string[] args)
    {
      Console.WriteLine("\nBegin data encoding and normalization demo\n");

      string[] sourceData = new string[] {
        "Sex    Age  Locale    Income      Politics",
        "==================================================",
        "Male    25  Rural     63,000.00   Conservative",
        "Female  36  Suburban  55,000.00   Liberal",
        "Male    40  Urban     74,000.00   Moderate",
        "Female  23  Rural     28,000.00   Liberal" };

      Console.WriteLine("Dummy data in raw form:\n");
      ShowData(sourceData);
```

```
        string[] encodedData = new string[] {
          "-1  25    1   0   63,000.00    1 0 0",
          " 1  36    0   1   55,000.00    0 1 0",
          "-1  40   -1  -1   74,000.00    0 0 1",
          " 1  23    1   0   28,000.00    0 1 0" };

        //Encode("..\\..\\Politics.txt", "..\\..\\PoliticsEncoded.txt", 4, "dummy");

        Console.WriteLine("\nData after categorical encoding:\n");
        ShowData(encodedData);

        Console.WriteLine("\nNumeric data stored in matrix:\n");
        double[][] numericData = new double[4][];
        numericData[0] = new double[] { -1, 25.0,  1,  0, 63000.00, 1, 0, 0 };
        numericData[1] = new double[] {  1, 36.0,  0,  1, 55000.00, 0, 1, 0 };
        numericData[2] = new double[] { -1, 40.0, -1, -1, 74000.00, 0, 0, 1 };
        numericData[3] = new double[] {  1, 23.0,  1,  0, 28000.00, 0, 1, 0 };

        ShowMatrix(numericData, 2);

        GaussNormal(numericData, 1);
        MinMaxNormal(numericData, 4);

        Console.WriteLine("\nMatrix after normalization (Gaussian col. 1" +
          " and MinMax col. 4):\n");
        ShowMatrix(numericData, 2);

        Console.WriteLine("\nEnd data encoding and normalization demo\n");
        Console.ReadLine();

      } // Main

      static void GaussNormal(double[][] data, int column)
      {
        int j = column; // Convenience.
        double sum = 0.0;
        for (int i = 0; i < data.Length; ++i)
          sum += data[i][j];
        double mean = sum / data.Length;

        double sumSquares = 0.0;
        for (int i = 0; i < data.Length; ++i)
          sumSquares += (data[i][j] - mean) * (data[i][j] - mean);
        double stdDev = Math.Sqrt(sumSquares / data.Length);

        for (int i = 0; i < data.Length; ++i)
          data[i][j] = (data[i][j] - mean) / stdDev;
      }

      static void MinMaxNormal(double[][] data, int column)
      {
        int j = column;
        double min = data[0][j];
        double max = data[0][j];
        for (int i = 0; i < data.Length; ++i)
        {
          if (data[i][j] < min)
            min = data[i][j];
          if (data[i][j] > max)
            max = data[i][j];
```

```csharp
      }
      double range = max - min;
      if (range == 0.0) // ugly
      {
        for (int i = 0; i < data.Length; ++i)
          data[i][j] = 0.5;
        return;
      }

      for (int i = 0; i < data.Length; ++i)
        data[i][j] = (data[i][j] - min) / range;
    }

    static void ShowMatrix(double[][] matrix, int decimals)
    {
      for (int i = 0; i < matrix.Length; ++i)
      {
        for (int j = 0; j < matrix[i].Length; ++j)
        {
          double v = Math.Abs(matrix[i][j]);
          if (matrix[i][j] >= 0.0)
            Console.Write(" ");
          else
            Console.Write("-");
          Console.Write(v.ToString("F" + decimals).PadRight(5) + " ");
        }
        Console.WriteLine("");
      }
    }

    static void ShowData(string[] rawData)
    {
      for (int i = 0; i < rawData.Length; ++i)
        Console.WriteLine(rawData[i]);
      Console.WriteLine("");
    }

    //static void EncodeFile(string originalFile, string encodedFile, int column,
    //  string encodingType)
    //{
    //  // encodingType: "effects" or "dummy"
    //  FileStream ifs = new FileStream(originalFile, FileMode.Open);
    //  StreamReader sr = new StreamReader(ifs);
    //  string line = "";
    //  string[] tokens = null;

    //  // count distinct items in column
    //  Dictionary<string, int> d = new Dictionary<string,int>();
    //  int itemNum = 0;
    //  while ((line = sr.ReadLine()) != null)
    //  {
    //    tokens = line.Split(','); // Assumes items are comma-delimited.
    //    if (d.ContainsKey(tokens[column]) == false)
    //      d.Add(tokens[column], itemNum++);
    //  }
    //  sr.Close();
    //  ifs.Close();

    //  // Replace items in the column.
    //  int N = d.Count; // Number of distinct strings.
```

```
//  ifs = new FileStream(originalFile, FileMode.Open);
//  sr = new StreamReader(ifs);

//  FileStream ofs = new FileStream(encodedFile, FileMode.Create);
//  StreamWriter sw = new StreamWriter(ofs);
//  string s = null; // result string/line
//  while ((line = sr.ReadLine()) != null)
//  {
//    s = "";
//    tokens = line.Split(','); // Break apart.
//    for (int i = 0; i < tokens.Length; ++i) // Reconstruct.
//    {
//      if (i == column) // Encode this string.
//      {
//        int index = d[tokens[i]]; // 0, 1, 2 or . .
//        if (encodingType == "effects")
//          s += EffectsEncoding(index, N) + ",";
//        else if (encodingType == "dummy")
//          s += DummyEncoding(index, N) + ",";
//      }
//      else
//        s += tokens[i] +",";
//    }
//    s.Remove(s.Length - 1); // Remove trailing ','.
//    sw.WriteLine(s); // Write the string to file.
//  } // while

//  sw.Close(); ofs.Close();
//  sr.Close(); ifs.Close();
//}

static string EffectsEncoding(int index, int N)
{
  // If N = 3 and index = 0 -> 1,0.
  // If N = 3 and index = 1 -> 0,1.
  // If N = 3 and index = 2 -> -1,-1.

  if (N == 2) // Special case.
  {
    if (index == 0) return "-1";
    else if (index == 1) return "1";
  }

  int[] values = new int[N - 1];
  if (index == N - 1) // Last item is all -1s.
  {
    for (int i = 0; i < values.Length; ++i)
      values[i] = -1;
  }
  else
  {
    values[index] = 1; // 0 values are already there.
  }

  string s = values[0].ToString();
  for (int i = 1; i < values.Length; ++i)
    s += "," + values[i];
  return s;
}
```

```
    static string DummyEncoding(int index, int N)
    {
      int[] values = new int[N];
      values[index] = 1;

      string s = values[0].ToString();
      for (int i = 1; i < values.Length; ++i)
        s += "," + values[i];
      return s;
    }

  } // Program class
} // ns
```

Chapter 2 Perceptrons

Introduction

A perceptron is software code that models the behavior of a single biological neuron. Perceptrons were one of the earliest forms of machine learning and can be thought of as the predecessors to neural networks. The types of neural networks described in this book are also known as multilayer perceptrons. Understanding exactly what perceptrons are and how they work is almost universal for anyone who works with machine learning. Additionally, although the types of problems that can be solved using perceptrons are quite limited, an understanding of perceptrons is very helpful when learning about neural networks, which are essentially collections of perceptrons.

The best way to get a feel for where this chapter is headed is to take a look at the screenshot of a demo program shown in **Figure 2-a**. The image shows a console application which implements a perceptron classifier. The goal of the classifier is to predict a person's political inclination, liberal or conservative, based on his or her age and income. The demo begins by setting up eight dummy training data items:

```
1.5   2.0   ->   -1
2.0   3.5   ->   -1
3.0   5.0   ->   -1
3.5   2.5   ->   -1
4.5   5.0   ->    1
5.0   7.0   ->    1
5.5   8.0   ->    1
6.0   6.0   ->    1
```

The first data item can be interpreted to mean that a person whose age is 1.5 and whose income is 2.0 is known to be a liberal (-1). Here, age has been normalized in some way, for example by dividing actual age in years by 10 and then subtracting 0.5, so 1.5 corresponds to a person who is 20 years old. Similarly, the person represented by the first data item has had his or her income normalized in some way. The purpose of normalizing each x-data feature is to make the magnitudes of all the features relatively the same. In this case, all are between 1.0 and 10.0. Experience has shown that normalizing input data often improves the accuracy of the resulting perceptron classifier. Notice that the dummy data items have been constructed so that persons with low age and low income values are liberal, and those with high age and high income are conservative.

The first person's political inclination is liberal, which has been encoded as -1. Conservative inclination is encoded as +1 in the training data. An alternative is to encode liberal and conservative as 0 and 1 respectively. Data normalization and encoding is an important topic in machine learning and is explained in <u>Chapter 1</u>. Because the variable to predict, political inclination, can have two possible values, liberal or conservative, the demo problem is called a binary classification problem.

```
file:///F:/Data/NeuralNetworksSuccinctly/Code/Chapter2/Perceptrons/bin/D...  _ □ ×

Begin perceptron demo

Predict liberal (-1) or conservative (+1) from age, income

The training data is:

[ 0]       1.5    2.0  ->  -1
[ 1]       2.0    3.5  ->  -1
[ 2]       3.0    5.0  ->  -1
[ 3]       3.5    2.5  ->  -1
[ 4]       4.5    5.0  ->  +1
[ 5]       5.0    7.0  ->  +1
[ 6]       5.5    8.0  ->  +1
[ 7]       6.0    6.0  ->  +1

Creating perceptron

Setting learning rate to 0.001 and maxEpochs to 100

Begin training
Training complete

Best weights and bias found:
 0.0045  0.0033 -0.0326

Predictions for new people:

Age, Income  =  3.0  4.0       Prediction is (-1) liberal
Age, Income  =  0.0  1.0       Prediction is (-1) liberal
Age, Income  =  2.0  5.0       Prediction is (-1) liberal
Age, Income  =  5.0  6.0       Prediction is (+1) conservative
Age, Income  =  9.0  9.0       Prediction is (+1) conservative
Age, Income  =  4.0  6.0       Prediction is (+1) conservative

End perceptron demo
-
```

Figure 2-a: Perceptron Demo Program

After setting up the eight dummy training data items, the demo creates a perceptron with a learning rate parameter that has a value of 0.001 and a maxEpochs parameter that has a value of 100. The learning rate controls how fast the perceptron will learn. The maxEpochs parameter controls how long the perceptron will learn. Next, behind the scenes, the perceptron uses the training data to learn how to classify. When finished, the result is a pair of weights with values 0.0045 and 0.0033, and a bias value of -0.0326. These weights and bias values essentially define the perceptron model.

After training, the perceptron is presented with six new data items where the political inclination is not known. The perceptron classifies each new person as either liberal or conservative. Notice that those people with low age and income were classified as liberal, and those with high age and income were classified as conservative. For example, the second unknown data item with age = 0.0 and income = 1.0 was classified as -1, which represents liberal.

Overall Demo Program Structure

The overall structure of the demo program is presented in **Listing 2-a**. To create the program, I launched Visual Studio and selected the console application project template. The program has no significant .NET Framework version dependencies so any version of Visual Studio should work. I named the project Perceptrons. After the Visual Studio template code loaded into the editor, I removed all using statements except for the one that references the top-level System namespace. In the Solution Explorer window, I renamed the Program.cs file to the more descriptive PerceptronProgram.cs, and Visual Studio automatically renamed the Program class for me.

```
using System;
namespace Perceptrons
{
  class PerceptronProgram
  {
    static void Main(string[] args)
    {
      Console.WriteLine("\nBegin perceptron demo\n");
      Console.WriteLine("Predict liberal (-1) or conservative (+1) from age, income");
      // Create and train perceptron.
      Console.WriteLine("\nEnd perceptron demo\n");
      Console.ReadLine();
    }

    static void ShowData(double[][] trainData) { . . }
    static void ShowVector(double[] vector, int decimals, bool newLine) { . . }
  }

  public class Perceptron
  {
    // Fields and methods are defined here.
  }
}
```

Listing 2-a: Overall Program Structure

The program class houses the Main method and two utility methods, ShowData and ShowVector. All the program logic is contained in a program-defined Perceptron class. Although it is possible to implement a perceptron using only static methods, using an object-oriented approach leads to much cleaner code in my opinion. The demo program has normal error-checking code removed in order to keep the main ideas as clear as possible.

The Input-Process-Output Mechanism

The perceptron input-process-output mechanism is illustrated in the diagram in **Figure 2-b**. The diagram corresponds to the first prediction in **Figure 2-a** where the inputs are age = x_0 = 3.0 and income = x_1 = 4.0, and the weights and bias values determined by the training process are w_0 = 0.0065, w_1 = 0.0123, and b= -0.0906 respectively. The first step in computing a perceptron's output is to sum the product of each input and the input's associated weight:

sum = (3.0)(0.0065) + (4.0)(0.0123) = 0.0687

The next step is to add the bias value to the sum:

sum = 0.0687 + (-0.0906) = -0.0219

The final step is to apply what is called an activation function to the sum. Activation functions are sometimes called transfer functions. There are several different types of activation functions. The demo program's perceptron uses the simplest type which is a step function where the output is +1 if the computed sum is greater than or equal to 0.0, or -1 if the computed sum is less than 0.0. Because the sum is -0.0219, the activation function gives -1 as the perceptron output, which corresponds to a class label of "liberal".

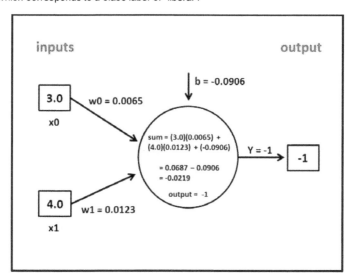

Figure 2-b: Perceptron Input-Output Mechanism

The input-process-output mechanism loosely models a single biological neuron. Each input value represents either a sensory input or the output value from some other neuron. The step function activation mimics the behavior of certain biological neurons which either fire or do not, depending on whether the weighted sum of input values exceeds some threshold.

One factor that can cause great confusion for beginners is the interpretation of the bias value. A perceptron bias value is just a constant that is added to the processing sum before the activation function is applied. Instead of treating the bias as a separate constant, many references treat the bias as a special type of weight with an associated dummy input value of 1.0. For example, in **Figure 2-b**, imagine that there is a third input node with value 1.0 and that the bias value b is now labeled as w_2. The sum would be computed as:

sum = (3.0)(0.0065) + (4.0)(0.0123) + (1.0)(-0.0906) = -0.0219 which is exactly the same result as before. Treating the bias as a special weight associated with a dummy input value of 1.0 is a common approach in research literature because the technique simplifies several mathematical proofs. However, treating the bias as a special weight has two drawbacks. First, the idea is somewhat unappealing intellectually. In my opinion, a constant bias term is clearly, conceptually distinct from a weight associated with an input because the bias models a real neuron's firing threshold value. Second, treating a bias as a special weight introduces the minor possibility of a coding error because the dummy input value can be either the first input (x_0 in the demo) or the last input (x_2).

The Perceptron Class Definition

The structure of the Perceptron class is presented in **Listing 2-b**. The integer field numInput holds the number of x-data features. For example, in the demo program, numInput would be set to 2 because there are two predictor variables, age and income.

The type double array field named "inputs" holds the values of the x-data. The double array field named "weights" holds the values of the weights associated with each input value both during and after training. The double field named "bias" is the value added during the computation of the perceptron output. The integer field named "output" holds the computed output of the perceptron. Field "rnd" is a .NET Random object which is used by the Perceptron constructor and during the training process.

```
public class Perceptron
{
  private int numInput;
  private double[] inputs;
  private double[] weights;
  private double bias;
  private int output;
  private Random rnd;

  public Perceptron(int numInput) { . . }
  private void InitializeWeights() { . . }
  public int ComputeOutput(double[] xValues) { . . }
  private static int Activation(double v) { . . }
  public double[] Train(double[][] trainData, double alpha, int maxEpochs) { . . }
  private void Shuffle(int[] sequence) { . . }
  private void Update(int computed, int desired, double alpha) { . .
}
```

Listing 2-b: The Perceptron Class

The Perceptron class exposes three public methods: a class constructor, method Train, and method ComputeOutput. The class has four private helper methods: method InitializeWeights is called by the class constructor, method Activation is called by ComputeOutput, and methods Shuffle and Update are called by Train.

The Perceptron class constructor is defined:

```
public Perceptron(int numInput)
{
  this.numInput = numInput;
  this.inputs = new double[numInput];
  this.weights = new double[numInput];
  this.rnd = new Random(0);
  InitializeWeights();
}
```

The constructor accepts the number of x-data features as input parameter numInput. That value is used to instantiate the class inputs array and weights array. The constructor instantiates the rnd Random object using a hard-coded value of 0 for the seed. An alternative is to pass the seed value as an input parameter to the constructor. In general, instantiating a Random object with a fixed seed value is preferable to calling the constructor overload with no parameter because a fixed seed allows you to reproduce training runs.

The constructor code finishes by calling private helper method InitializeWeights. Method InitializeWeights assigns a different, small random value between -0.01 and +0.01 to each perceptron weight and the bias. The method is defined as:

```
private void InitializeWeights()
{
  double lo = -0.01;
  double hi = 0.01;
  for (int i = 0; i < weights.Length; ++i)
    weights[i] = (hi - lo) * rnd.NextDouble() + lo;
  bias = (hi - lo) * rnd.NextDouble() + lo;
}
```

The random interval of [-0.01, +0.01] is hard-coded. An alternative is to pass one or both interval end points to InitializeWeights as parameters. This approach would require you to either make the scope of InitializeWeights public so that the method can be called separately from the constructor, or to add the interval end points as parameters to the constructor so that they can be passed to InitializeWeights.

The ComputeOutput Method

Public method ComputeOutput accepts an array of input values and uses the perceptron's weights and bias values to generate the perceptron output. Method ComputeOutput is presented in **Listing 2-c**.

```
public int ComputeOutput(double[] xValues)
{
  if (xValues.Length != numInput)
    throw new Exception("Bad xValues in ComputeOutput");
  for (int i = 0; i < xValues.Length; ++i)
    this.inputs[i] = xValues[i];
  double sum = 0.0;
  for (int i = 0; i < numInput; ++i)
```

```
    sum += this.inputs[i] * this.weights[i];
  sum += this.bias;
  int result = Activation(sum);
  this.output = result;
  return result;
}
```

Listing 2-c: ComputeOutput Method

After a check to verify that the size of the input array parameter is correct, the method copies the values in the array parameter into the class inputs array. Because method ComputeOutput will typically be called several hundred or thousand times during the training process, an alternative design approach is to eliminate the class inputs array field and compute output directly from the x-values array parameter. This alternative approach is slightly more efficient but a bit less clear than using an explicit inputs array.

Method ComputeOutput computes a sum of the products of each input and its associated weight, adds the bias value, and then applies the step activation function. An alternative design is to delete the simple activation method definition and place the activation code logic directly into method ComputeOutput. However, a separate activation method has the advantage of being a more modular design and emphasizing the separate nature of the activation function.

The step activation function is defined as:

```
private static int Activation(double v)
{
  if (v >= 0.0)
    return +1;
  else
    return -1;
}
```

Recall that the demo problem encodes the two y-values to predict as -1 for liberal and +1 for conservative. If you use a 0-1 encoding scheme you would have to modify method Activation to return those two values.

Training the Perceptron

Training a perceptron is the process of iteratively adjusting the weights and bias values so that the computed outputs for a given set of training data x-values closely match the known outputs. Expressed in high-level pseudo-code, the training process is:

```
loop
  for each training item
    compute output using x-values
    compare computed output to known output
    if computed is too large
      make weights and bias values smaller
    else if computed is too small
      make weights and bias values larger
    end if
```

```
  end for
end loop
```

Although training is fairly simple conceptually, the implementation details are a bit tricky. Method Train is presented in **Listing 2-d**. Method Train accepts as input parameters a matrix of training data, a learning rate alpha, and a loop limit maxEpochs. Experience has shown that in many situations it is preferable to iterate through the training data items using a random order each time through the main processing loop rather than using a fixed order. To accomplish this, method Train uses an array named sequence. Each value in array sequence represents an index into the row of the training data. For example, the demo program has eight training items. If array sequence held values { 7, 1, 0, 6, 4, 3, 5, 2 }, then row 7 of the training data would be processed first, row 1 would be processed second, and so on.

Helper method Shuffle is defined as:

```
private void Shuffle(int[] sequence)
{
  for (int i = 0; i < sequence.Length; ++i)
  {
    int r = rnd.Next(i, sequence.Length);
    int tmp = sequence[r];
    sequence[r] = sequence[i];
    sequence[i] = tmp;
  }
}
```

Method Shuffle uses the Fisher-Yates algorithm to scramble the values in its array parameter. The key to the training algorithm is the helper method Update, presented in **Listing 2-e**. Method Update accepts a computed output value, the desired output value from the training data, and a learning rate alpha. Recall that computed and desired output values are either -1 (for liberal) or +1 (for conservative).

```
public double[] Train(double[][] trainData, double alpha, int maxEpochs)
{
  int epoch = 0;
  double[] xValues = new double[numInput];
  int desired = 0;

  int[] sequence = new int[trainData.Length];
  for (int i = 0; i < sequence.Length; ++i)
    sequence[i] = i;

  while (epoch < maxEpochs)
  {
    Shuffle(sequence);
    for (int i = 0; i < trainData.Length; ++i)
    {
      int idx = sequence[i];
      Array.Copy(trainData[idx], xValues, numInput);
      desired = (int)trainData[idx][numInput]; // -1 or +1.
      int computed = ComputeOutput(xValues);
      Update(computed, desired, alpha); // Modify weights and bias values
    } // for each data.
    ++epoch;
  }
```

```
    double[] result = new double[numInput + 1];
    Array.Copy(this.weights, result, numInput);
    result[result.Length - 1] = bias; // Last cell.
    return result;
}
```

Listing 2-d: The Train Method

Method Update calculates the difference between the computed output and the desired output and stores the difference into the variable delta. Delta will be positive if the computed output is too large, or negative if computed output is too small. For a perceptron with -1 and +1 outputs, delta will always be either -2 (if computed = -1 and desired = +1), or +2 (if computed = +1 and desired = -1), or 0 (if computed equals desired).

For each weight[i], if the computed output is too large, the weight is reduced by amount (alpha * delta * input[i]). If input[i] is positive, the product term will also be positive because alpha and delta are also positive, and so the product term is subtracted from weight[i]. If input[i] is negative, the product term will be negative, and so to reduce weight[i] the product term must be added.

Notice that the size of the change in a weight is proportional to both the magnitude of delta and the magnitude of the weight's associated input value. So a larger delta produces a larger change in weight, and a larger associated input also produces a larger weight change.

The learning rate alpha scales the magnitude of a weight change. Larger values of alpha generate larger changes in weight which leads to faster learning, but at a risk of overshooting a good weight value. Smaller values of alpha avoid overshooting but make training slower.

```
private void Update(int computed, int desired, double alpha)
{
  if (computed == desired) return; // We're good.
  int delta = computed - desired;  // If computed > desired, delta is +.

  for (int i = 0; i < this.weights.Length; ++i) // Each input-weight pair.
  {
    if (computed > desired && inputs[i] >= 0.0) // Need to reduce weights.
      weights[i] = weights[i] - (alpha * delta * inputs[i]); // delta is +, input is +
    else if (computed > desired && inputs[i] < 0.0) // Need to reduce weights.
      weights[i] = weights[i] + (alpha * delta * inputs[i]); // delta is +, input is -
    else if (computed < desired && inputs[i] >= 0.0) // Need to increase weights.
      weights[i] = weights[i] - (alpha * delta * inputs[i]); // delta is -, input is +
    else if (computed < desired && inputs[i] < 0.0) // Need to increase weights.
      weights[i] = weights[i] + (alpha * delta * inputs[i]); // delta is -, input is -
  } // Each weight.
  bias = bias - (alpha * delta);
}
```

Listing 2-e: The Update Method

The weight adjustment logic leads to four control branches in method Update, depending on whether delta is positive or negative, and whether input[i] is positive or negative. Inputs are assumed to not be zero so you might want to check for this. In pseudo-code:

```
if computed > desired and input > 0 then
  weight = weight - (alpha * delta * input)
else if computed > desired and input < 0 then
  weight = weight + (alpha * delta * input)
else if computed < desired and input > 0 then
  weight = weight - (alpha * delta * input)
else if  computed < desired and input < 0 then
  weight = weight + (alpha * delta * input)
end if
```

If you examine the logic closely you can see that the first and third branches, and the second and fourth branches can be combined so the previous pseudo-code is equivalent to:

```
if input > 0 then
  weight = weight - (alpha * delta * input)
else
  weight = weight + (alpha * delta * input)
end if
```

And, in situations where the input data has been normalized so that all values are non-negative, the update logic can be condensed even further, like so:

```
weight = weight - (alpha * delta * input) /* assumes input > 0 */
```

In my opinion, the four-branch logic is the most clear but least efficient, and the single-branch logic is most efficient but least clear. In most cases, the performance impact of the four-branch logic will not be significant.

Updating the bias value does not depend on the value of an associated input, so the logic is:

```
if computed > desired then
  bias = bias - (alpha * delta)
else
  bias = bias - (alpha * delta)
end if
```

Therefore, the code logic can be simplified to just:

```
bias = bias - (alpha * delta)
```

Notice that all the update logic depends on the way in which delta is computed. The demo arbitrarily computes delta as (computed - desired). If you choose to compute delta as (desired - computed) then you would have to adjust the update code logic appropriately.

The learning rate alpha and the loop count limit maxEpochs are sometimes called free parameters. These are values that must be supplied by the user. The term free parameters is also used to refer to the perceptron's weights and bias because these values are free to vary during training. In general, the best choice of values for perceptron and neural network free parameters such as the learning rate must be found by trial and error experimentation. This unfortunate characteristic is common to many forms of machine learning.

Using the Perceptron Class

The key statements in the Main method of the demo program which create and train the perceptron are:

```
int numInput = 2;
Perceptron p = new Perceptron(numInput);
double alpha = 0.001;
int maxEpochs = 100;
double[] weights = p.Train(trainData, alpha, maxEpochs);
```

The interface is very simple; first a perceptron is created and then it is trained. The final weights and bias values found during training are returned by the Train method. An alternative design is to implement a property GetWeights and call along the lines of:

```
double alpha = 0.001;
int maxEpochs = 100;
p.Train(trainData, alpha, maxEpochs);
double[] weights = p.GetWeights();
```

The code for the Main method of the demo program is presented in **Listing 2-f**. The training data is hard-coded:

```
double[][] trainData = new double[8][];
trainData[0] = new double[] { 1.5, 2.0, -1 };
// etc.
```

```
static void Main(string[] args)
{
    Console.WriteLine("\nBegin perceptron demo\n");
    Console.WriteLine("Predict liberal (-1) or conservative (+1) from age, income");

    double[][] trainData = new double[8][];
    trainData[0] = new double[] { 1.5, 2.0, -1 };
    trainData[1] = new double[] { 2.0, 3.5, -1 };
    trainData[2] = new double[] { 3.0, 5.0, -1 };
    trainData[3] = new double[] { 3.5, 2.5, -1 };
    trainData[4] = new double[] { 4.5, 5.0, 1 };
    trainData[5] = new double[] { 5.0, 7.0, 1 };
    trainData[6] = new double[] { 5.5, 8.0, 1 };
    trainData[7] = new double[] { 6.0, 6.0, 1 };

    Console.WriteLine("\nThe training data is:\n");
    ShowData(trainData);
    Console.WriteLine("\nCreating perceptron");
    int numInput = 2;
    Perceptron p = new Perceptron(numInput);

    double alpha = 0.001;
    int maxEpochs = 100;
    Console.Write("\nSetting learning rate to " + alpha.ToString("F3"));
    Console.WriteLine(" and maxEpochs to " + maxEpochs);

    Console.WriteLine("\nBegin training");
    double[] weights = p.Train(trainData, alpha, maxEpochs);

    Console.WriteLine("Training complete");
```

```
    Console.WriteLine("\nBest weights and bias found:");
    ShowVector(weights, 4, true);

    double[][] newData = new double[6][];
    newData[0] = new double[] { 3.0, 4.0 }; // Should be -1.
    newData[1] = new double[] { 0.0, 1.0 }; // Should be -1.
    newData[2] = new double[] { 2.0, 5.0 }; // Should be -1.
    newData[3] = new double[] { 5.0, 6.0 }; // Should be 1.
    newData[4] = new double[] { 9.0, 9.0 }; // Should be 1.
    newData[5] = new double[] { 4.0, 6.0 }; // Should be 1.

    Console.WriteLine("\nPredictions for new people:\n");
    for (int i = 0; i < newData.Length; ++i)
    {
      Console.Write("Age, Income = ");
      ShowVector(newData[i], 1, false);
      int c = p.ComputeOutput(newData[i]);
      Console.Write("   Prediction is ");
      if (c == -1)
        Console.WriteLine("(-1) liberal");
      else if (c == 1)
        Console.WriteLine("(+1) conservative");
    }

    Console.WriteLine("\nEnd perceptron demo\n");
    Console.ReadLine();
}
```

Listing 2-f: The Main Method

In many situations, training data is stored externally, for example in a text file or SQL database. In these situations you will have to write a utility method to load the data into memory along the lines of:

```
string dataLocation = "C:\\Data\\AgeIncome.txt";
double[][] trainData = LoadData(dataLocation);
```

The perceptron demo program has two helper methods, ShowData and ShowVector, to display the contents of the training data matrix and the contents of an array of type double. The code for these two helper methods is presented in **Listing 2-g**.

```
static void ShowData(double[][] trainData)
{
  int numRows = trainData.Length;
  int numCols = trainData[0].Length;
  for (int i = 0; i < numRows; ++i)
  {
    Console.Write("[" + i.ToString().PadLeft(2, ' ') + "]   ");
    for (int j = 0; j < numCols - 1; ++j)
      Console.Write(trainData[i][j].ToString("F1").PadLeft(6));
    Console.WriteLine("   ->   " + trainData[i][numCols - 1].ToString("+0;-0"));
  }
}

static void ShowVector(double[] vector, int decimals, bool newLine)
{
  for (int i = 0; i < vector.Length; ++i)
  {
```

```
    if (vector[i] >= 0.0)
      Console.Write(" "); // For sign.
    Console.Write(vector[i].ToString("F" + decimals) + " ");
  }
  if (newLine == true)
    Console.WriteLine("");
}
```

Listing 2-g: Helper Methods ShowData and ShowVector

Making Predictions

In the Main method, after the perceptron has been instantiated and trained to classify a person's political inclination based on his or her age and income, the perceptron is presented with six new data items where the political inclination is not known:

```
double[][] newData = new double[6][];
newData[0] = new double[] { 3.0, 4.0 }; // Output should be -1.
newData[1] = new double[] { 0.0, 1.0 }; // Should be -1.
newData[2] = new double[] { 2.0, 5.0 }; // Should be -1.
newData[3] = new double[] { 5.0, 6.0 }; // Should be 1.
newData[4] = new double[] { 9.0, 9.0 }; // Should be 1.
newData[5] = new double[] { 4.0, 6.0 }; // Should be 1.
```

The key code to predict political inclination for newData item [i] is:

```
int c = p.ComputeOutput(newData[i]);
Console.Write("Prediction is ");
if (c == -1)
  Console.WriteLine("(-1) liberal");
else if (c == 1)
  Console.WriteLine("(+1) conservative");
```

After training, the perceptron holds weights and bias values that generate computed y-value outputs that closely match the known y-value outputs of the training data. These weights and bias values are used by method ComputeOutput to generate a -1 or +1 output.

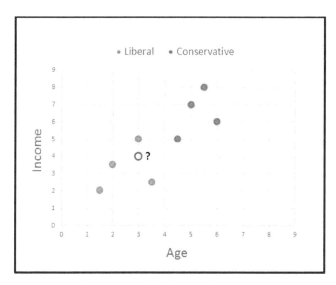

Figure 2-c: Predicting Liberal or Conservative

The graph in **Figure 2-c** illustrates how perceptron prediction works. The green and red dots are the training data. The open blue dot with the question mark is newData[0] where age is 3.0 and income is 4.0 (normalized). From the graph, it's pretty obvious that the new person is more likely liberal (green) than conservative (red).

Training a perceptron essentially finds a straight line so that all the training data items in one class (for example, liberal in the demo) are on one side of the line and all the items in the other class (conservative) are on the other side of the line. This characteristic of perceptrons is called linear separability. Notice that there are many possible separating lines.

Limitations of Perceptrons

Soon after the first perceptrons were studied in the 1950s, it became clear that perceptrons have several weaknesses that limit their usefulness to only simple classification problems.

Because perceptrons essentially find a separating line between training data y-value classes, perceptrons can only make good predictions in situations where this is possible.

Put slightly differently, suppose that in **Figure 2-c** the training data were positioned in such a way that there was a clear distinction between liberal and conservative, but the dividing space between classes was a curved, rather than straight, line. A simple perceptron would be unable to handle such a situation. In general, with real-life data it's not possible to know in advance whether the training data is linearly separable or not.

Another weakness of the perceptron implementation presented here is related to the training process. In the demo, the training loop executes a fixed number of times specified by the maxEpochs variable. What is really needed is a measure of error so that training can be stopped when the overall error drops below some threshold value. As it turns out, the notion of a training error term is closely related to the activation function. The demo perceptron uses a simple step function which does not lend itself well to an error function. The limitations of the simple perceptron model gave rise to neural networks in the 1980s.

Neural networks have two main enhancements over perceptrons. First, a neural network has many processing nodes, instead of just one, which are organized into two layers. This is why neural networks are sometimes called multilayer perceptrons. Second, neural networks typically use activation functions which are more sophisticated than the step function typically used by perceptrons. Both enhancements increase the processing power of neural networks relative to perceptrons.

In the late 1980s, neural network research proved that, loosely speaking, a fully connected feed-forward neural network that uses a sophisticated activation function can approximate any continuous mathematical function. This is called the universal approximation theorem, or sometimes the Cybenko theorem. What this means is that neural networks can accurately classify data if it is possible to separate the y-data using any smooth, curved line or surface.

For example, take another look at the graph of political inclination based on age and income in **Figure 2-c**. A perceptron can only classify correctly when it is possible to draw a straight line on the graph so that all the conservative data points are on one side of the line and all the liberal data points are on the other side. But a neural network can classify correctly when it is possible to draw any smooth, curved line to separate the two classes.

Complete Demo Program Source Code

```
using System;
namespace Perceptrons
{
  class PerceptronProgram
  {
    static void Main(string[] args)
    {
      Console.WriteLine("\nBegin perceptron demo\n");
      Console.WriteLine("Predict liberal (-1) or conservative (+1) from age, income");

      double[][] trainData = new double[8][];
      trainData[0] = new double[] { 1.5, 2.0, -1 };
      trainData[1] = new double[] { 2.0, 3.5, -1 };
      trainData[2] = new double[] { 3.0, 5.0, -1 };
      trainData[3] = new double[] { 3.5, 2.5, -1 };
      trainData[4] = new double[] { 4.5, 5.0, 1 };
      trainData[5] = new double[] { 5.0, 7.0, 1 };
      trainData[6] = new double[] { 5.5, 8.0, 1 };
      trainData[7] = new double[] { 6.0, 6.0, 1 };

      Console.WriteLine("\nThe training data is:\n");
      ShowData(trainData);
```

```
      Console.WriteLine("\nCreating perceptron");
      int numInput = 2;
      Perceptron p = new Perceptron(numInput);

      double alpha = 0.001;
      int maxEpochs = 100;

      Console.Write("\nSetting learning rate to " + alpha.ToString("F3"));
      Console.WriteLine(" and maxEpochs to " + maxEpochs);

      Console.WriteLine("\nBegin training");
      double[] weights = p.Train(trainData, alpha, maxEpochs);

      Console.WriteLine("Training complete");
      Console.WriteLine("\nBest weights and bias found:");
      ShowVector(weights, 4, true);

      double[][] newData = new double[6][];
      newData[0] = new double[] { 3.0, 4.0 }; // Should be -1.
      newData[1] = new double[] { 0.0, 1.0 }; // Should be -1.
      newData[2] = new double[] { 2.0, 5.0 }; // Should be -1.
      newData[3] = new double[] { 5.0, 6.0 }; // Should be 1.
      newData[4] = new double[] { 9.0, 9.0 }; // Should be 1.
      newData[5] = new double[] { 4.0, 6.0 }; // Should be 1.

      Console.WriteLine("\nPredictions for new people:\n");
      for (int i = 0; i < newData.Length; ++i)
      {
        Console.Write("Age, Income = ");
        ShowVector(newData[i], 1, false);
        int c = p.ComputeOutput(newData[i]);
        Console.Write("   Prediction is ");
        if (c == -1)
          Console.WriteLine("(-1) liberal");
        else if (c == 1)
          Console.WriteLine("(+1) conservative");
      }

      Console.WriteLine("\nEnd perceptron demo\n");
      Console.ReadLine();
    } // Main

    static void ShowData(double[][] trainData)
    {
      int numRows = trainData.Length;
      int numCols = trainData[0].Length;
      for (int i = 0; i < numRows; ++i)
      {
        Console.Write("[" + i.ToString().PadLeft(2, ' ') + "] ");
        for (int j = 0; j < numCols - 1; ++j)
          Console.Write(trainData[i][j].ToString("F1").PadLeft(6));
        Console.WriteLine("  -> " + trainData[i][numCols - 1].ToString("+0;-0"));
      }
    }

    static void ShowVector(double[] vector, int decimals, bool newLine)
    {
      for (int i = 0; i < vector.Length; ++i)
      {
        if (vector[i] >= 0.0)
          Console.Write(" "); // For sign.
```

```
      Console.Write(vector[i].ToString("F" + decimals) + " ");
    }
    if (newLine == true)
      Console.WriteLine("");
  }
} // Program

public class Perceptron
{
  private int numInput;
  private double[] inputs;
  private double[] weights;
  private double bias;
  private int output;
  private Random rnd;

  public Perceptron(int numInput)
  {
    this.numInput = numInput;
    this.inputs = new double[numInput];
    this.weights = new double[numInput];
    this.rnd = new Random(0);
    InitializeWeights();
  }

  private void InitializeWeights()
  {
    double lo = -0.01;
    double hi = 0.01;
    for (int i = 0; i < weights.Length; ++i)
      weights[i] = (hi - lo) * rnd.NextDouble() + lo;
    bias = (hi - lo) * rnd.NextDouble() + lo;
  }

  public int ComputeOutput(double[] xValues)
  {
    if (xValues.Length != numInput)
      throw new Exception("Bad xValues in ComputeOutput");
    for (int i = 0; i < xValues.Length; ++i)
      this.inputs[i] = xValues[i];
    double sum = 0.0;
    for (int i = 0; i < numInput; ++i)
      sum += this.inputs[i] * this.weights[i];
    sum += this.bias;
    int result = Activation(sum);
    this.output = result;
    return result;
  }

  private static int Activation(double v)
  {
    if (v >= 0.0)
      return +1;
    else
      return -1;
  }

  public double[] Train(double[][] trainData, double alpha, int maxEpochs)
  {
    int epoch = 0;
    double[] xValues = new double[numInput];
```

```
      int desired = 0;

      int[] sequence = new int[trainData.Length];
      for (int i = 0; i < sequence.Length; ++i)
        sequence[i] = i;

      while (epoch < maxEpochs)
      {
        Shuffle(sequence);
        for (int i = 0; i < trainData.Length; ++i)
        {
          int idx = sequence[i];
          Array.Copy(trainData[idx], xValues, numInput);
          desired = (int)trainData[idx][numInput]; // -1 or +1.
          int computed = ComputeOutput(xValues);
          Update(computed, desired, alpha); // Modify weights and bias values
        } // for each data.
        ++epoch;
      }

      double[] result = new double[numInput + 1];
      Array.Copy(this.weights, result, numInput);
      result[result.Length - 1] = bias; // Last cell.
      return result;
    } // Train

    private void Shuffle(int[] sequence)
    {
      for (int i = 0; i < sequence.Length; ++i)
      {
        int r = rnd.Next(i, sequence.Length);
        int tmp = sequence[r];
        sequence[r] = sequence[i];
        sequence[i] = tmp;
      }
    }

    private void Update(int computed, int desired, double alpha)
    {
      if (computed == desired) return; // We're good.
      int delta = computed - desired;  // If computed > desired, delta is +.
      for (int i = 0; i < this.weights.Length; ++i) // Each input-weight pair.
      {
        if (computed > desired && inputs[i] >= 0.0) // Need to reduce weights.
          weights[i] = weights[i] - (alpha * delta * inputs[i]); // delta +, alpha +, input

        else if (computed > desired && inputs[i] < 0.0) // Need to reduce weights.
          weights[i] = weights[i] + (alpha * delta * inputs[i]); // delta +, alpha +, input

        else if (computed < desired && inputs[i] >= 0.0) // Need to increase weights.
          weights[i] = weights[i] - (alpha * delta * inputs[i]); // delta -, aplha +, input

        else if (computed < desired && inputs[i] < 0.0) // Need to increase weights.
          weights[i] = weights[i] + (alpha * delta * inputs[i]); // delta -, alpha +, input


        // Logically equivalent:
        //If (inputs[i] >= 0.0) // Either reduce or increase weights (depending on delta).
        //  weights[i] = weights[i] - (alpha * delta * inputs[i]);
        //else
        //  weights[i] = weights[i] + (alpha * delta * inputs[i]);
```

```
        // Also equivalent if all input > 0, but not obvious.
        //weights[i] = weights[i] - (alpha * delta * inputs[i]);

    } // Each weight.

    bias = bias - (alpha * delta);

    }
  } // Perceptron
} // ns
```

Chapter 3 Feed-Forward

Introduction

A neural network is essentially a mathematical function that accepts one or more numeric inputs and produces one or more numeric outputs. The basic neural network input-process-output computation is called the feed-forward mechanism. Understanding the feed-forward mechanism is essential to understanding how to create neural networks that can make predictions.

The best way to get a feel for where this chapter is headed is to take a look at the screenshot of a demo program shown in **Figure 3-a** and the associated diagram in **Figure 3-b**. Both figures illustrate the same dummy neural network with three inputs and two outputs. The dummy input values are 1.0, 2.0, and 3.0, and the output values generated are 0.4920 and 0.5080. The demo neural network has an internal layer of four hidden nodes. The neural network has 26 constants called weights and biases that are used during the computation of the output values.

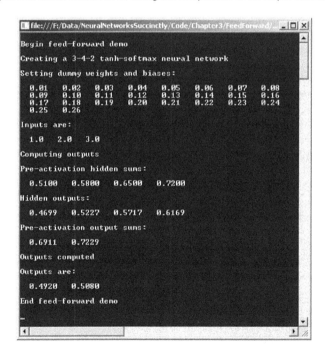

Figure 3-a: Feed-Forward Mechanism Demo

The demo program in **Figure 3-a** displays some intermediate values during the computation of the outputs. These intermediate values, the pre-activation hidden sums, hidden outputs, and pre-activation output sums normally would not be shown and are there just to help you understand the feed-forward mechanism.

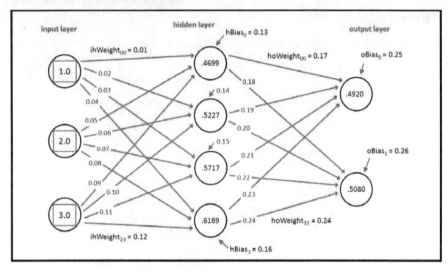

Figure 3-b: Neural Network Architecture

Understanding Feed-Forward

A neural network computes its outputs in several steps and the feed-forward mechanism is best explained using a concrete example. In **Figure 3-b**, there are three dummy inputs with values 1.0, 2.0, and 3.0. In the figure, objects are zero-based indexed, from top to bottom, so the top-most input with value 1.0 is inputs[0] and the bottom-most input with value 3.0 is inputs[2].

Each red line connecting one node to another represents a weight constant. The top-most weight with value 0.01 is labeled ihWeight[0][0], which means the weight from input node 0 to hidden node 0. Similarly, the weight in the lower right corner of **Figure 3-b**, with value 0.24, is labeled hoWeight[3][1] which means the weight from hidden node 3 to output node 1.

Each of the hidden and output layer nodes has an arrow pointing to it. These are called the bias values. The bias value at the top of the figure with value 0.13 is labeled hBias[0] which means the bias value for hidden node 0.

The first step in the feed-forward mechanism is to compute the values shown in the hidden layer nodes. The value of hidden node 0 is 0.4699 and is computed as follows. First, the product of each input value and its associated weight are summed:

hSums[0] = (1.0)(0.01) + (2.0)(0.05) + (3.0)(0.09) = 0.01 + 0.10 + 0.27 = 0.38

Next, the associated bias value is added:

hSums[0] = 0.38 + 0.13 = 0.51

In **Figure 3-a**, you can see this displayed as the first pre-activation sum. Next, a so-called activation function is applied to the sum. Activation functions will be explained in detail later, but for now it's enough to say that the activation function is the hyperbolic tangent function, which is usually abbreviated tanh.

hOutputs[0] = tanh(0.51) = 0.4699

You can see the 0.4699 displayed as the first hidden output in **Figure 3-a**, and also as the value inside the top-most hidden node in **Figure 3-b**. The other three hidden nodes are computed in the same way. Here, the steps are combined to save space:

hOutputs[1] = tanh((1.0)(0.02) + (2.0)(0.06) + (3.0)(0.10) + 0.14) = tanh(0.58) = 0.5227
hOutputs[2] = tanh((1.0)(0.03) + (2.0)(0.07) + (3.0)(0.11) + 0.15) = tanh(0.65) = 0.5717
hOutputs[3] = tanh((1.0)(0.04) + (2.0)(0.08) + (3.0)(0.12) + 0.16) = tanh(0.72) = 0.6169

After all hidden node output values have been computed, these values are used as inputs to the output layer. The output node values are computed slightly differently from the hidden nodes. The preliminary output sums, before activation, for output nodes 0 and 1 are computed the same way as the preliminary hidden node sums, by summing products of inputs and weights and then adding a bias value:

oSums[0] = (0.4699)(0.17) + (0.5227)(0.19) + (0.5717)(0.21) + (0.6169)(0.23) + 0.25 = 0.6911
oSums[1] = (0.4699)(0.18) + (0.5227)(0.20) + (0.5717)(0.22) + (0.6169)(0.24) + 0.26 = 0.7229

The activation function for the output layer is called the softmax function. This will be explained later, but for now the softmax of each preliminary sum is best explained by example:

output[0] = exp(0.6911) / (exp(0.6911) + exp(0.7229)) = 1.9959 / (1.9959 + 2.0604) = 0.4920
output[1] = exp(0.7229) / (exp(0.6911) + exp(0.7229)) = 2.0604 / (1.9959 + 2.0604) = 0.5080

If you look at both **Figures 3-a** and **3-b**, you will see these are the final output values computed by the demo neural network. Here, the exp function of some value x is the math constant e = 2.71828. . . raised to the xth power. Notice the two output values sum to 1.0, which is not a coincidence and is the point of using the softmax function.

To summarize, a neural network is essentially a mathematical function whose outputs are determined by the input values, a number of hidden nodes, a set of weights and bias values, and two activation functions. The architecture presented here is called a fully-connected network, because the nodes in a given layer are connected to all the nodes in the next layer. It is possible to design neural networks that are not fully connected.

Bias Values as Special Weights

When working with neural networks, you must pay careful attention to how the bias values are handled. In the previous section, bias values are treated as distinct constants. However, the majority of neural network research treats biases as special weights associated with a dummy input value of 1.0.

For example, in **Figure 3-b**, the bias value for hidden node 0 is 0.13. The pre-activation sum for hidden node 0, if the bias is treated as a true bias, is computed as:

hSum[0] = (1.0)(0.01) + (2.0)(0.05) + (3.0)(0.09) + 0.13 = 0.51

If you imagine a dummy input node with the value 1.0 next to hidden node 0, and consider the bias as a special weight, the pre-activation sum would be computed as:

hSum[0] = (1.0)(0.01) + (2.0)(0.05) + (3.0)(0.09) + (1.0)(0.13) = 0.51

In other words, the result is the same. The point of treating a bias as a special weight is that doing so simplifies many of the mathematical proofs and derivations in research. But from a developer's point of view, treating a bias as a special weight is conceptually awkward and, in my opinion, more error-prone than treating all biases as true biases.

Overall Demo Program Structure

The overall structure of the demo program is presented in **Listing 3-a**. After the Visual Studio template code loaded into the editor, I removed all using statements except for the one that references the top-level System namespace. In the Solution Explorer window, I renamed the Program.cs file to the more descriptive FeedForwardProgram.cs, and Visual Studio automatically renamed the Program class for me.

```
using System;
namespace FeedForward
{
  class FeedForwardProgram
  {
    static void Main(string[] args)
    {
      Console.WriteLine("\nBegin feed-forward demo\n");

      int numInput = 3;
      int numHidden = 4;
      int numOutput = 2;

      Console.WriteLine("Creating a 3-4-2 tanh-softmax neural network");
      NeuralNetwork nn = new NeuralNetwork(numInput, numHidden, numOutput);
      // Set weights.
      // Set inputs.
      // Compute and display outputs.

      Console.WriteLine("\nEnd feed-forward demo\n");
      Console.ReadLine();
    }
```

```
    public static void ShowVector(double[] vector, int valsPerRow,
      int decimals, bool newLine) { . . }
  } // Program

  public class NeuralNetwork { . . }

}
```

Listing 3-a: Overall Program Structure

The program class houses the Main method and a utility method ShowVector. All the program logic is contained in a program-defined NeuralNetwork class. Although it is possible to implement a neural network using only arrays and static methods, using an object-oriented approach leads to easier-to-understand code in my opinion. The demo program has most normal error checking removed in order to keep the main ideas as clear as possible.

The Main method begins by instantiating the demo neural network:

```
static void Main(string[] args)
{
  Console.WriteLine("\nBegin feed-forward demo\n");
  int numInput = 3;
  int numHidden = 4;
  int numOutput = 2;
  Console.WriteLine("Creating a 3-4-2 tanh-softmax neural network");
  NeuralNetwork nn = new NeuralNetwork(numInput, numHidden, numOutput);
```

Notice that the demo neural network constructor accepts parameter values for the number of input nodes, the number of hidden nodes, and the number of output nodes. This means that the two activation functions used, tanh and softmax, are hardwired into the network.

The demo program continues by setting up 26 dummy weights and bias values and then placing them into the neural network using a method SetWeights:

```
double[] weights = new double[] {
  0.01, 0.02, 0.03, 0.04, 0.05, 0.06, 0.07, 0.08, 0.09, 0.10,
  0.11, 0.12, 0.13, 0.14, 0.15, 0.16, 0.17, 0.18, 0.19, 0.20,
  0.21, 0.22, 0.23, 0.24, 0.25, 0.26
};

Console.WriteLine("\nSetting dummy weights and biases:");
ShowVector(weights, 8, 2, true);
nn.SetWeights(weights);
```

If you refer to the diagram in **Figure 3-b** you can see the relationship between the architecture of a neural network and the number of weights and bias values. Because there is a weight from each input node to each hidden node, there are (numInput * numHidden) input-to-hidden weights. Each hidden node has a bias value so there are numHidden hidden node biases. There is a weight from each hidden node to each output node, making (numHidden * numOutput) weights. And each output node has a bias making numOutput more biases. Putting this all together, there are a total of (numInput * numHidden) + numHidden + (numHidden * numOutput) + numOutput weights and bias values.

Next, the demo sets up and displays three arbitrary input values:

```
double[] xValues = new double[] { 1.0, 2.0, 3.0 };
Console.WriteLine("\nInputs are:");
ShowVector(xValues, 3, 1, true);
```

The demo program concludes by computing and displaying the output values:

```
  Console.WriteLine("\nComputing outputs");
  double[] yValues = nn.ComputeOutputs(xValues);
  Console.WriteLine("\nOutputs computed");
  Console.WriteLine("\nOutputs are:");
  ShowVector(yValues, 2, 4, true);
  Console.WriteLine("\nEnd feed-forward demo\n");
  Console.ReadLine();
} // Main
```

The code for utility method ShowVector is:

```
public static void ShowVector(double[] vector, int valsPerRow,
  int decimals, bool newLine)
{
  for (int i = 0; i < vector.Length; ++i)
  {
    if (i % valsPerRow == 0)
      Console.WriteLine("");
    Console.Write(vector[i].ToString("F" + decimals).PadLeft(decimals + 4) + " ");
  }
  if (newLine == true)
    Console.WriteLine("");
}
```

The ShowVector method is declared with public scope so that it can be called inside methods in the NeuralNetwork class.

Designing the Neural Network Class

There are many ways to implement a neural network in code. The design presented in **Listing 3-b** emphasizes simplicity over efficiency. Member fields numInput, numHidden, and numOutput store the number of input nodes, hidden nodes, and output nodes. The array member named inputs holds the numeric inputs to the neural network. Interestingly, as will be shown shortly, the inputs array can be omitted for slightly increased processing efficiency.

Matrix member ihWeights holds the weights from input nodes to hidden nodes, where the row index corresponds to the index of an input node, and the column index corresponds to the index of a hidden node. The matrix is implemented as an array of arrays. Unlike most programming languages, C# has a true multidimensional array and you may want to use that approach to store the neural network weights.

Member array hBiases holds the bias values for the hidden nodes. Many implementations you'll find will omit this array and instead treat the hidden node biases as extra input-to-hidden weights.

Member array hOutputs stores the hidden node outputs after summing the products of weights and inputs, adding the bias value, and applying an activation function during the computation of the output values. An alternative is to make this array local to the ComputeOutputs. However, because in most situations the ComputeOutputs method is called many thousands of times, a local array would have to be allocated many times. Naming array hOutputs is a bit tricky because the values also serve as inputs to the output layer.

Member matrix hoWeights holds the weights from hidden nodes to output nodes. The row index of the matrix corresponds to the index of a hidden node and the column index corresponds to the index of an output node.

Member array oBiases holds bias values for the output nodes. The member array named outputs holds the final overall computed neural network output values. As with the inputs array, you'll see that the outputs array can potentially be dropped from the design.

```
public class NeuralNetwork
{
    private int numInput;
    private int numHidden;
    private int numOutput;

    private double[] inputs;

    private double[][] ihWeights;
    private double[] hBiases;
    private double[] hOutputs;

    private double[][] hoWeights;
    private double[] oBiases;

    private double[] outputs;

    public NeuralNetwork(int numInput, int numHidden, int numOutput) { . . }
    private static double[][] MakeMatrix(int rows, int cols) { . . }
    public void SetWeights(double[] weights) { . . }
    public double[] ComputeOutputs(double[] xValues) { . . }
    private static double HyperTan(double v) { . . }
    private static double[] Softmax(double[] oSums) { . . }
}
```

Listing 3-b: Designing a Neural Network Class

The neural network class in **Listing 3-b** has three public methods: a constructor, a method to set the values of the weights and biases, and a method that computes and returns the output values. In later chapters, as training features are added to the neural network, additional public-scope methods will be added to the class definition.

Private method MakeMatrix is a helper method called by the constructor. Private helper methods HyperTan and Softmax are called by method ComputeOutputs.

The Neural Network Constructor

The NeuralNetwork class constructor begins by copying each input parameter value to its associated member field:

```
public NeuralNetwork(int numInput, int numHidden, int numOutput)
{
  this.numInput = numInput;
  this.numHidden = numHidden;
  this.numOutput = numOutput;
```

Next, space for the inputs array is allocated:

```
this.inputs = new double[numInput];
```

Next, the constructor allocates space for the input-to-hidden weights matrix using helper method MakeMatrix:

```
this.ihWeights = MakeMatrix(numInput, numHidden);
```

An alternative is to allocate the matrix directly, but using a helper method makes sense here because the helper can be reused when allocating the hidden-to-output weights matrix. Method MakeMatrix is defined as:

```
private static double[][] MakeMatrix(int rows, int cols)
{
  double[][] result = new double[rows][];
  for (int i = 0; i < rows; ++i)
    result[i] = new double[cols];
  return result;
}
```

Depending on your background, you may be unfamiliar with working with C# array-of-arrays style matrices. The matrix syntax does not correspond closely to most normal programming idioms and can take a while to get accustomed to.

The NeuralNetwork class constructor finishes by allocating space for the remaining member matrix and four arrays:

```
  this.hBiases = new double[numHidden];
  this.hOutputs = new double[numHidden];
  this.hoWeights = MakeMatrix(numHidden, numOutput);
  this.oBiases = new double[numOutput];
  this.outputs = new double[numOutput];
}
```

Setting Neural Network Weights and Bias Values

The demo program uses a method SetWeights to populate weight matrices ihWeights and hoWeights, and bias arrays hBiases and oBiases with values. Method SetWeights is presented in **Listing 3-c**. Method SetWeights accepts a single array parameter which holds all the weights and bias values.

The method assumes that the values in the weights array parameter are stored in a particular order: first the input-to-hidden weights, followed by the hidden biases, followed by the hidden-to-output weights, followed by the output biases. Additionally, the values for the two weights matrices are assumed to be stored in row-major order. This means the values are ordered from left to right and top to bottom.

As usual, a concrete example is the best way to explain. The demo neural network shown in **Figure 3-b** was created by passing an array with values { 0.01, 0.02, 0.03, . . 0.26 } to the SetWeights method. This populates matrix ihWeights with values:

```
0.01   0.02   0.03   0.04
0.05   0.06   0.07   0.08
0.09   0.10   0.11   0.12
```

The hBiases array gets:

```
0.13   0.14   0.15   0.16
```

Matrix hoWeights gets:

```
0.17   0.18
0.19   0.20
0.21   0.22
0.23   0.24
```

And the oBiases array gets:

```
0.25   0.26
```

This assumption of a particular ordering of the values in the array parameter passed to method SetWeights is somewhat brittle. The alternative is to explicitly pass two matrices and two arrays to SetWeights, but in my opinion, the extra complexity outweighs the increased safety unless you were designing your neural network for use by others.

```
public void SetWeights(double[] weights)
{
    int numWeights = (numInput * numHidden) + numHidden +
      (numHidden * numOutput) + numOutput;
    if (weights.Length != numWeights)
        throw new Exception("Bad weights array");

    int k = 0; // Pointer into weights parameter.

    for (int i = 0; i < numInput; ++i)
      for (int j = 0; j < numHidden; ++j)
        ihWeights[i][j] = weights[k++];
```

```
    for (int i = 0; i < numHidden; ++i)
      hBiases[i] = weights[k++];

    for (int i = 0; i < numHidden; ++i)
      for (int j = 0; j < numOutput; ++j)
        hoWeights[i][j] = weights[k++];

    for (int i = 0; i < numOutput; ++i)
      oBiases[i] = weights[k++];
}
```

Listing 3-c: Setting Weights and Bias Values

Computing Outputs

Method ComputeOutputs implements the feed-forward mechanism. The method, with diagnostic WriteLine statements removed, is presented in **Listing 3-d**. The method definition begins by doing a simple check on the input values:

```
public double[] ComputeOutputs(double[] xValues)
{
  if (xValues.Length != numInput)
    throw new Exception("Bad xValues array");
```

In a realistic neural network scenario, you might want to consider dropping this input parameter check to improve performance. An alternative is to pass in a Boolean flag parameter named something like checkInput to indicate whether or not to perform the error check; however, in this case checking the value of the Boolean would incur as much overhead as performing the error check itself.

```
public double[] ComputeOutputs(double[] xValues)
{
  if (xValues.Length != numInput)
    throw new Exception("Bad xValues array");

  double[] hSums = new double[numHidden];
  double[] oSums = new double[numOutput];

  for (int i = 0; i < xValues.Length; ++i)
    inputs[i] = xValues[i];

  for (int j = 0; j < numHidden; ++j)
    for (int i = 0; i < numInput; ++i)
      hSums[j] += inputs[i] * ihWeights[i][j];

  for (int i = 0; i < numHidden; ++i)
    hSums[i] += hBiases[i];

  for (int i = 0; i < numHidden; ++i)
    hOutputs[i] = HyperTan(hSums[i]);

  for (int j = 0; j < numOutput; ++j)
    for (int i = 0; i < numHidden; ++i)
      oSums[j] += hSums[i] * hoWeights[i][j];
```

```
    for (int i = 0; i < numOutput; ++i)
      oSums[i] += oBiases[i];

    double[] softOut = Softmax(oSums); // Softmax does all outputs at once.
    for (int i = 0; i < outputs.Length; ++i)
      outputs[i] = softOut[i];

    double[] result = new double[numOutput];
    for (int i = 0; i < outputs.Length; ++i)
      result[i] = outputs[i];

    return result;
  }
```

Listing 3-d: Computing Neural Network Output Values

Next, method ComputeOutputs creates and allocates scratch arrays to hold the pre-activation sum of products of inputs and weights plus a bias value:

```
double[] hSums = new double[numHidden];
double[] oSums = new double[numOutput];
```

Recall that in C#, when an array of type double is created, the cell values are automatically set to 0.0. As mentioned previously, in most situations, when a neural network is being trained, the feed-forward mechanism is called many thousands of times. So, at first thought, the alternative of declaring the two arrays as class-scope fields rather than repeatedly allocating the two scratch sum arrays inside method ComputeOutputs is appealing. However, this has the downside of cluttering up the class definition. Additionally, because these scratch arrays hold accumulations of sums, the array would have to be zeroed-out at the beginning of ComputeOutputs, which negates most of the advantage of not having to allocate the arrays.

Next, the input values are copied from the xValues array parameter into the member inputs array:

```
for (int i = 0; i < xValues.Length; ++i)
  inputs[i] = xValues[i];
```

A syntactic alternative is to use the C# Array.Copy method. If you review the feed-forward mechanism carefully, you'll see that the values in the member array named inputs are used but not changed. Therefore it is possible to eliminate the inputs array and just use the values in the xValues array. Because method ComputeOutputs might be called thousands or even millions of times depending upon the usage scenario, eliminating an unnecessary array copy could save significant time.

Eliminating the inputs member array has at least two disadvantages, however. First, conceptually, a neural network does have inputs and so eliminating them just doesn't feel quite right in some subjective way. Second, if you implement a class ToString method, you'd certainly want to be able to see the current values of the inputs which would not be possible if the inputs array is not in the class definition.

An alternative is to pass a Boolean flag parameter named copyInputs to the method ComputeOutputs along the lines of:

```
public double[] ComputeOutputs(double[] xValues, bool copyInputs)
{
  if (copyInputs == true)
  {
    for (int i = 0; i < xValues.Length; ++i)
      inputs[i] = xValues[i];
  }
  else
    inputs = xValues;
```

Using this approach would improve performance at the minor risk of a possible unwanted side effect; in the else-branch when parameter copyInputs is false, the inputs array is assigned a reference (essentially a pointer) to the xValues array. Any change to one of the arrays effectively changes the other array. In short, explicitly copying the xValues array values to the inputs member array is safer and clearer but has slower performance than implicitly copying using a reference.

After copying values into the inputs member array, method ComputeOutputs accumulates the sum of products of input-to-hidden weights and inputs:

```
for (int j = 0; j < numHidden; ++j)
  for (int i = 0; i < numInput; ++i)
    hSums[j] += inputs[i] * ihWeights[i][j];
```

Although short, the code is somewhat tricky because of the array indexing. In this case, index j points into the hidden sums array and also acts as the column index into the input-to-hidden weights matrix. As a general rule, based on my experience, most of the bugs in my neural network implementations are related to array and matrix indexing. Developers have different approaches to coding, but for me, drawing pictures of my arrays and matrices and indices, using paper and pencil, is the only way I can keep my indices correct.

Next, the bias values are added to the accumulated hidden node sums:

```
for (int i = 0; i < numHidden; ++i)
  hSums[i] += hBiases[i];

Console.WriteLine("\nPre-activation hidden sums:");
FeedForwardProgram.ShowVector(hSums, 4, 4, true);
```

In the demo program, the hidden sums are displayed only for informational purposes. In a realistic, non-demo scenario these sums would not be displayed. One common approach is to pass in a Boolean parameter, often named "verbose", to control whether or not to print diagnostic messages.

Next, the hyperbolic tangent activation function is applied to each sum to give the hidden node's output values:

```
for (int i = 0; i < numHidden; ++i)
  hOutputs[i] = HyperTan(hSums[i]);

Console.WriteLine("\nHidden outputs:");
FeedForwardProgram.ShowVector(hOutputs, 4, 4, true);
```

Activation functions will be discussed in detail in the following section of this chapter. For now, notice that the HyperTan function accepts a single value of type double and returns a single value of type double. Therefore, the function must be applied individually to each hidden sum.

Next, method ComputeOutputs computes the pre-activation sums for the output layer nodes:

```
for (int j = 0; j < numOutput; ++j)
  for (int i = 0; i < numHidden; ++i)
    oSums[j] += hOutputs[i] * hoWeights[i][j];

for (int i = 0; i < numOutput; ++i)
  oSums[i] += oBiases[i];

Console.WriteLine("\nPre-activation output sums:");
FeedForwardProgram.ShowVector(oSums, 2, 4, true);
```

Next, softmax activation is applied to the sums and the final results are stored into the outputs array:

```
double[] softOut = Softmax(oSums);
  for (int i = 0; i < outputs.Length; ++i)
    outputs[i] = softOut[i];
```

Notice that unlike the HyperTan method, method Softmax accepts an array of double values and returns an array of double values.

Method ComputeOutputs finishes by copying the values in the class member array named outputs to a local method return result array and then returning that array:

```
  double[] result = new double[numOutput];
  for (int i = 0; i < outputs.Length; ++i)
    result[i] = outputs[i];

  return result;
} // ComputeOutputs
```

In effect, method ComputeOutputs returns the output values of the neural network in two ways: first, stored into class member array outputs, and second, as an explicit return value. This idea is a bit subtle and is mostly for calling flexibility. Explicitly returning the neural network outputs allows you to fetch the outputs into an array with a call like:

```
double[] yValues = nn.ComputeOutputs(xValues);
```

The output values also reside in the neural network object, so if you implement a GetOutputs method you could make a call along the lines of:

```
nn.ComputeOutputs(xValues);
double[] yValues = nn.GetOutputs();
```

One possible implementation of a GetOutputs method is:

```
public double[] GetOutputs()
{
  double[] result = new double[numOutput];
  for (int i = 0; i < numOutput; ++i)
    result[i] = this.outputs[i];
  return result;
}
```

Activation Functions

The demo program uses the hyperbolic tangent function for hidden layer node activation and the softmax function for output layer node activation. There is a third common activation function called the logistic sigmoid function. All three of these activation functions are closely related mathematically. From a developer's point of view, you need to know two things: when to use each activation function and how to implement each function.

Although there are some exceptions, in general the hyperbolic tangent function is the best choice for hidden layer activation. For output layer activation, if your neural network is performing classification where the dependent variable to be predicted has three or more values (for example, predicting a person's political inclination which can be "liberal", "moderate", or "conservative"), softmax activation is the best choice. If your neural network is performing classification where the dependent variable has exactly two possible values (for example, predicting a person's gender which can be "male" or "female"), the logistic sigmoid activation function is the best choice for output layer activation. Chapter 5 explains the details.

In the demo program, the hyperbolic tangent function is defined as:

```
private static double HyperTan(double v)
{
  if (v < -20.0)
    return -1.0;
  else if (v > 20.0)
    return 1.0;
  else
    return Math.Tanh(v);
}
```

Here the neural network HyperTan method is essentially a wrapper around the built-in .NET Tanh function. To better understand method HyperTan, take a look at the graph of the hyperbolic tangent shown in **Figure 3-c**. The Tanh function accepts any numeric value from negative infinity to positive infinity, and returns a value between -1.0 and +1.0. For example, Tanh(2.0) = 0.9640 and Tanh(-3.0) = -0.9951. Notice that for x values smaller than about -8.0 and larger than +8.0, the Tanh function result gets extremely close to -1 and +1 respectively.

Most programming languages, including C#, have a built-in hyperbolic tangent function. But in the early days of neural network research, some older programming languages had difficulty computing the hyperbolic tangent function for very small or very large input parameters. So, it was common to perform the kind of parameter check used in the HyperTan method.

The logistic sigmoid function, also called log-sigmoid, is similar to the hyperbolic tangent function. The logistic sigmoid function accepts any numeric value from negative infinity to positive infinity, and returns a value between 0.0 and +1.0. Unlike the hyperbolic tangent, most programming languages do not have a built-in logistic sigmoid function. The math definition of the logistic sigmoid function is: $f(x) = 1 / (1 + e^{-x})$.

Most programming languages, including C#, have a built-in function, usually named Exp, that returns e raised to a power. So, one possible implementation of the logistic sigmoid function is:

```
private static double LogSigmoid(double x)
{
  if (x < -45.0)
    return 0.0;
  else if (x > 45.0)
    return 1.0;
  else
    return 1.0 / (1.0 + Math.Exp(-x));
}
```

The input parameter check values of -45.0 and +45.0 are traditional values. On old computing hardware and software, the computation of Math.Exp(-x) could cause arithmetic overflow when x was very large or small, so the standard approach was to use an input parameter check.

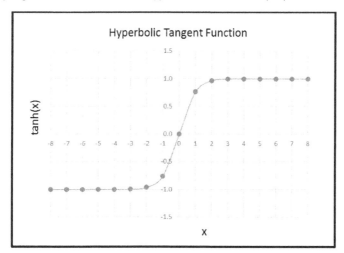

Figure 3-c: The Hyperbolic Tangent Function

The softmax activation function is a variation of the logistic sigmoid function. The logistic sigmoid function accepts a single value and returns a single value between 0.0 and 1.0. The softmax activation function accepts n values and returns a set of n values which sum to 1.0. For example, softmax of { 1.0, 4.0, 2.0 } returns { 0.04, 0.84, 0.12 }.

The mathematical definition of the softmax function is a bit difficult to express, so an example may be the best way to explain. Suppose there are three values, 1.0, 4.0, and 2.0.

softmax(1.0) = $e^{1.0}$ / ($e^{1.0}$ + $e^{4.0}$ + $e^{2.0}$) = 2.7183 / (2.7183 + 54.5982 + 7.3891) = 0.04

softmax(4.0) = $e^{4.0}$ / ($e^{1.0}$ + $e^{4.0}$ + $e^{2.0}$) = 54.5982 / (2.7183 + 54.5982 + 7.3891) = 0.84

softmax(2.0) = $e^{2.0}$ / ($e^{1.0}$ + $e^{4.0}$ + $e^{2.0}$) = 7.3891 / (2.7183 + 54.5982 + 7.3891) = 0.12

A possible naive implementation of softmax is:

```
public static double[] SoftmaxNaive(double[] values)
{
  double denom = 0.0;
  for (int i = 0; i < oSums.Length; ++i)
    denom += Math.Exp(oSums[i]);

  double[] result = new double[oSums.Length];
  for (int i = 0; i < oSums.Length; ++i)
    result[i] = Math.Exp(oSums[i]) / denom;
  return result;
}
```

The problem with the naive implementation of the softmax function is that the denominator term can easily get very large or very small and cause a potential arithmetic overflow. It is possible to implement a more sophisticated version of the softmax function by using some clever math. Again, the technique is best explained by an example.

Using the three values from the previous example, 1.0, 4.0, and 2.0, the first step is to determine the largest value, which in this case is max = 4.0. The next step is to compute a scaling factor which is the sum of e raised to each input value minus the maximum input value:

scale = $e^{(1.0 - max)}$ + $e^{(4.0 - max)}$ + $e^{(2.0 - max)}$ = $e^{-3.0}$ + e^{0} + $e^{-2.0}$ = 0.0498 + 1 + 0.1353 = 1.1851

The final softmax outputs are e raised to each input minus the maximum divided by the scaling factor:

softmax(1.0) = $e^{(1.0 - max)}$ / scale = $e^{-3.0}$ / 1.1851 = 0.0498 / 1.1851 = 0.04

softmax(4.0) = $e^{(4.0 - max)}$ / scale = e^{0} / 1.1851 = 1 / 1.1851 = 0.84

softmax(2.0) = $e^{(2.0 - max)}$ / scale = $e^{-2.0}$ / 1.1851 = 0.1353 / 1.1851 = 0.12

Notice that these are the same results as computed using the math definition. The reason why the two computation techniques give the same result isn't obvious, but is based on the property that $e^{(a-b)} = e^{a} / e^{b}$. The point of using the alternate computation technique is that the scaling process decreases the magnitude of each of the values that e is being raised to, which reduces the chances of arithmetic overflow. The demo program implementation of the softmax function is given in **Listing 3-e**.

```
public static double[] Softmax(double[] oSums)
{
  double max = oSums[0];
  for (int i = 0; i < oSums.Length; ++i)
    if (oSums[i] > max)
      max = oSums[i];

  double scale = 0.0;
  for (int i = 0; i < oSums.Length; ++i)
    scale += Math.Exp(oSums[i] - max);

  double[] result = new double[oSums.Length];
  for (int i = 0; i < oSums.Length; ++i)
    result[i] = Math.Exp(oSums[i] - max) / scale;

  return result; // Cell values sum to ~1.0.
}
```

Listing 3-e: The Softmax Activation Method

Because the softmax function is applied only to sums for output layer nodes, the method's input array parameter is named oSums rather than something more general like "values".

The demo program has hard-coded activation functions hyperbolic tangent for the hidden layer nodes, and softmax for the output layer nodes. An alternative is to pass some parameter information to the neural network constructor that indicates which activation function to use for each layer. This introduces additional complexity. As a rule of thumb, when I am developing code for my own use, I prefer simplicity over a more general solution. On the other hand, if you were developing neural network code for use by others, especially if you don't intend to make the source code available and editable, you'd have to take the general approach for dealing with activation functions.

There are many ways you could modify the neural network class presented here to handle parameterized activation functions. One approach is to define a class-scope enumeration type along with member fields, along the lines of:

```
public class NeuralNetwork
{
  public enum Activation { HyperTan, LogSigmoid, Softmax };
  private Activation hActivation;
  private Activation oActivation;
```

The constructor would accept additional parameters:

```
public NeuralNetwork(int numInput, int numHidden, int numOutput,
  Activation hActivation, Activation oActivation)
{
    this.numInput = numInput;
    this.numHidden = numHidden;
    this.numOutput = numOutput;
    this.hActivation = hActivation;
    this.oActivation = oActivation;
```

And the ComputeOutputs method could employ branching logic such as:

```
for (int i = 0; i < numHidden; ++i)
{
  if (this.hActivation == Activation.HyperTan)
    hOutputs[i] = HyperTan(hSums[i]);
  else if (this.hActivation == Activation.LogSigmoid)
    hOutputs[i] = LogSigmoid(hSums[i]);
}
```

The neural network constructor could then be called like:

```
NeuralNetwork nn = new NeuralNetwork(numInput, numHidden, numOutput,
  NeuralNetwork.Activation.HyperTan, NeuralNetwork.Activation.Softmax);
```

It should be apparent that designing a neural network to be general, typically for use by other developers, involves a lot of additional code. As you'll see in later chapters, there are dozens of ways to modify the behavior of a neural network. In general, I personally prefer to keep my neural network implementations as simple as possible and am willing to pay the price of having to modify source code often.

Complete Demo Program Source Code

```
using System;
namespace FeedForward
{
  class FeedForwardProgram
  {
    static void Main(string[] args)
    {
      Console.WriteLine("\nBegin feed-forward demo\n");

      int numInput = 3;
      int numHidden = 4;
      int numOutput = 2;

      Console.WriteLine("Creating a 3-4-2 tanh-softmax neural network");
      NeuralNetwork nn = new NeuralNetwork(numInput, numHidden, numOutput);

      double[] weights = new double[] { 0.01, 0.02, 0.03, 0.04,
        0.05, 0.06, 0.07, 0.08,
        0.09, 0.10, 0.11, 0.12,
        0.13, 0.14, 0.15, 0.16,
        0.17, 0.18, 0.19, 0.20,
        0.21, 0.22, 0.23, 0.24,
        0.25, 0.26 };

      Console.WriteLine("\nSetting dummy weights and biases:");
      ShowVector(weights, 8, 2, true);

      nn.SetWeights(weights);

      double[] xValues = new double[] { 1.0, 2.0, 3.0 };
      Console.WriteLine("\nInputs are:");
      ShowVector(xValues, 3, 1, true);

      Console.WriteLine("\nComputing outputs");
```

```csharp
      double[] yValues = nn.ComputeOutputs(xValues);
      Console.WriteLine("\nOutputs computed");

      Console.WriteLine("\nOutputs are:");
      ShowVector(yValues, 2, 4, true);

      Console.WriteLine("\nEnd feed-forward demo\n");
      Console.ReadLine();
    } // Main

    public static void ShowVector(double[] vector, int valsPerRow, int decimals, bool
newLine)
    {
      for (int i = 0; i < vector.Length; ++i)
      {
        if (i % valsPerRow == 0)
          Console.WriteLine("");
        Console.Write(vector[i].ToString("F" + decimals).PadLeft(decimals + 4) + " ");
      }
      if (newLine == true)
        Console.WriteLine("");
    }
  } // Program

  public class NeuralNetwork
  {
    private int numInput;
    private int numHidden;
    private int numOutput;

    private double[] inputs;

    private double[][] ihWeights;
    private double[] hBiases;
    private double[] hOutputs;

    private double[][] hoWeights;
    private double[] oBiases;
    private double[] outputs;

    public NeuralNetwork(int numInput, int numHidden, int numOutput)
    {
      this.numInput = numInput;
      this.numHidden = numHidden;
      this.numOutput = numOutput;

      this.inputs = new double[numInput];
      this.ihWeights = MakeMatrix(numInput, numHidden);
      this.hBiases = new double[numHidden];
      this.hOutputs = new double[numHidden];

      this.hoWeights = MakeMatrix(numHidden, numOutput);
      this.oBiases = new double[numOutput];
      this.outputs = new double[numOutput];
    }

    private static double[][] MakeMatrix(int rows, int cols)
    {
      double[][] result = new double[rows][];
      for (int i = 0; i < rows; ++i)
        result[i] = new double[cols];
```

```csharp
    return result;
}

public void SetWeights(double[] weights)
{
  int numWeights = (numInput * numHidden) + numHidden +
    (numHidden * numOutput) + numOutput;
  if (weights.Length != numWeights)
    throw new Exception("Bad weights array");

  int k = 0; // Pointer into weights.

  for (int i = 0; i < numInput; ++i)
    for (int j = 0; j < numHidden; ++j)
      ihWeights[i][j] = weights[k++];

  for (int i = 0; i < numHidden; ++i)
    hBiases[i] = weights[k++];

  for (int i = 0; i < numHidden; ++i)
    for (int j = 0; j < numOutput; ++j)
      hoWeights[i][j] = weights[k++];

  for (int i = 0; i < numOutput; ++i)
    oBiases[i] = weights[k++];
}

public double[] ComputeOutputs(double[] xValues)
{
  if (xValues.Length != numInput)
    throw new Exception("Bad xValues array");

  double[] hSums = new double[numHidden];
  double[] oSums = new double[numOutput];

  for (int i = 0; i < xValues.Length; ++i)
    inputs[i] = xValues[i];

// ex: hSum[0] = (in[0] * ihW[[0][0]) + (in[1] * ihW[1][0]) + (in[2] * ihW[2][0]) + . .
//     hSum[1] = (in[0] * ihW[[0][1]) + (in[1] * ihW[1][1]) + (in[2] * ihW[2][1]) + . .
//     . . .
  for (int j = 0; j < numHidden; ++j)
    for (int i = 0; i < numInput; ++i)
      hSums[j] += inputs[i] * ihWeights[i][j];

  for (int i = 0; i < numHidden; ++i)
    hSums[i] += hBiases[i];

  Console.WriteLine("\nPre-activation hidden sums:");
  FeedForwardProgram.ShowVector(hSums, 4, 4, true);

  for (int i = 0; i < numHidden; ++i)
    hOutputs[i] = HyperTan(hSums[i]);

  Console.WriteLine("\nHidden outputs:");
  FeedForwardProgram.ShowVector(hOutputs, 4, 4, true);

  for (int j = 0; j < numOutput; ++j)
    for (int i = 0; i < numHidden; ++i)
      oSums[j] += hOutputs[i] * hoWeights[i][j];
```

```
        for (int i = 0; i < numOutput; ++i)
          oSums[i] += oBiases[i];

        Console.WriteLine("\nPre-activation output sums:");
        FeedForwardProgram.ShowVector(oSums, 2, 4, true);

        double[] softOut = Softmax(oSums); // Softmax does all outputs at once.
        for (int i = 0; i < outputs.Length; ++i)
          outputs[i] = softOut[i];

        double[] result = new double[numOutput];
        for (int i = 0; i < outputs.Length; ++i)
          result[i] = outputs[i];

        return result;
    }

    private static double HyperTan(double v)
    {
      if (v < -20.0)
        return -1.0;
      else if (v > 20.0)
        return 1.0;
      else
        return Math.Tanh(v);
    }

    public static double[] Softmax(double[] oSums)
    {
      // Does all output nodes at once.
      // Determine max oSum.
      double max = oSums[0];
      for (int i = 0; i < oSums.Length; ++i)
        if (oSums[i] > max)
          max = oSums[i];

      // Determine scaling factor -- sum of exp(each val - max).
      double scale = 0.0;
      for (int i = 0; i < oSums.Length; ++i)
        scale += Math.Exp(oSums[i] - max);

      double[] result = new double[oSums.Length];
      for (int i = 0; i < oSums.Length; ++i)
        result[i] = Math.Exp(oSums[i] - max) / scale;

      return result; // Now scaled so that xi sums to 1.0.
    }

    public static double[] SoftmaxNaive(double[] oSums)
    {
      double denom = 0.0;
      for (int i = 0; i < oSums.Length; ++i)
        denom += Math.Exp(oSums[i]);

      double[] result = new double[oSums.Length];
      for (int i = 0; i < oSums.Length; ++i)
        result[i] = Math.Exp(oSums[i]) / denom;
      return result;
    }
  } // NeuralNetwork
} // ns
```

Chapter 4 Back-Propagation

Introduction

Back-propagation is an algorithm that can be used to train a neural network. Training a neural network is the process of finding a set of weights and bias values so that, for a given set of inputs, the outputs produced by the neural network are very close to some known target values. Once you have these weight and bias values, you can apply them to new input values where the output value is not known, and make a prediction. This chapter explains the back-propagation algorithm.

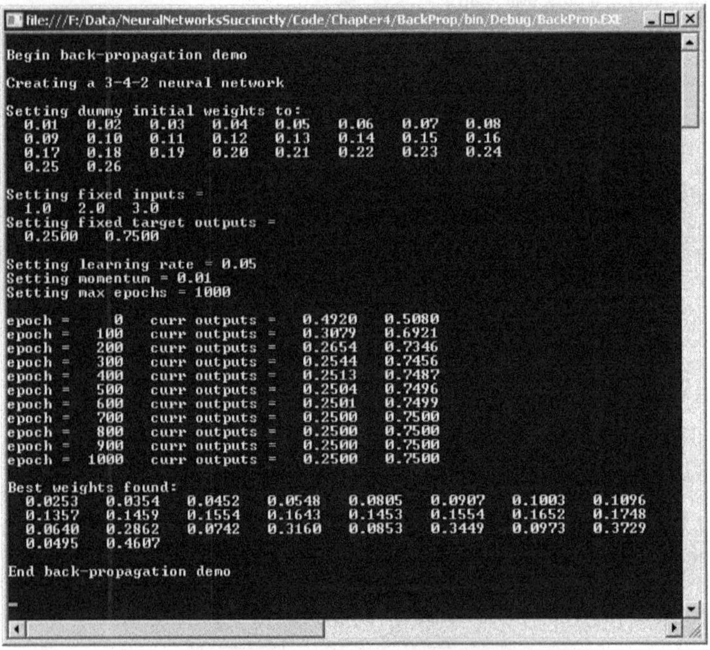

Figure 4-a: Back-Propagation Demo

There are alternatives to back-propagation (which is often spelled as the single word backpropagation), but back-propagation is by far the most common neural network training algorithm. A good way to get a feel for exactly what back-propagation is, is to examine the screenshot of a demo program shown in **Figure 4-a**. The demo program creates a dummy neural network with three inputs, four hidden nodes, and two outputs. The demo neural network does not correspond to a real problem and works on only a single data item.

The demo neural network has fixed, arbitrary input values of 1.0, 2.0, and 3.0. The goal of the demo program is to find a set of 26 weights and bias values so that the computed outputs are very close to arbitrary target output values of 0.2500 and 0.7500. Back-propagation is an iterative process. After 1,000 iterations, the demo program did in fact find a set of weight and bias values that generate output values which are very close to the two desired target values.

Back-propagation compares neural network computed outputs (for a given set of inputs, and weights and bias values) with target values, determines the magnitude and direction of the difference between actual and target values, and then adjusts the neural network's weights and bias values so that the new outputs will be closer to the target values. This process is repeated until the actual output values are close enough to the target values, or some maximum number of iterations has been reached.

The Basic Algorithm

There are many variations of the back-propagation algorithm. Expressed in high-level pseudo-code, basic back-propagation is:

```
loop until some exit condition
  compute output values
  compute gradients of output nodes
  compute gradients of hidden layer nodes
  update all weights and bias values
end loop
```

Gradients are values that reflect the difference between a neural network's computed output values and the desired target values. As it turns out, gradients use the calculus derivative of the associated activation function. The gradients of the output nodes must be computed before the gradients of the hidden layer nodes, or in other words, in the opposite direction of the feed-forward mechanism. This is why back-propagation, which is a shortened form of "backwards propagation", is named as it is. Unlike gradients which must be computed in a particular order, the output node weights and biases and the hidden layer node weights and biases can be updated in any order.

If you refer to the screenshot in **Figure 4-a**, you can see that back-propagation uses a learning rate parameter and a momentum parameter. Both of these values influence how quickly back-propagation converges to a good set of weights and bias values. Large values allow back-propagation to learn more quickly but at the risk of overshooting an optimal set of values. Determining good values for the learning rate and the momentum term is mostly a matter of trial and error. The learning rate and momentum term are called free parameters; you are free to set their values to whatever you choose. Weights and biases are also called free parameters.

Many neural network references state that back-propagation is a simple algorithm. This is only partially true. Once understood, back-propagation is relatively simple to implement in code. However, the algorithm itself is very deep. It took machine learning researchers many years to derive the basic back-propagation algorithm.

Computing Gradients

The first step in the back-propagation is to compute the values of the gradients for the output nodes. **Figure 4-b** represents the dummy 3-4-2 neural network of the demo program. The three fixed input values are 1.0, 2.0, and 3.0. The 26 weights and bias values are 0.01, 0.02, . . 0.26.

The current output values generated by the inputs and weights and bias values are 0.4920 and 0.5080. The neural network is using the hyperbolic tangent function for the hidden layer nodes and softmax activation for output layer nodes. The desired target values are 0.2500 and 0.7500.

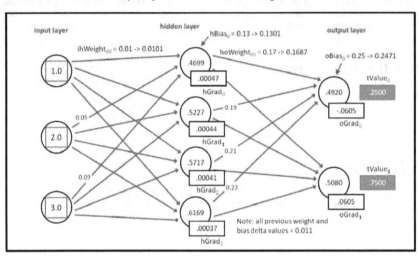

Figure 4-b: The Back-Propagation Mechanism

The gradient of an output node is the difference between the computed output value and the desired value, multiplied by the calculus derivative of the activation function used by the output layer. The difference term is reasonable but exactly why the calculus derivative term is used is not at all obvious and is a result of deep but beautiful mathematics.

The calculus derivative of the softmax activation function at some value y is just $y(1 - y)$. Again, this is not obvious and is part of the mathematics of neural networks. The values of the output node gradients are calculated as:

oGrad[0] = (1 - 0.4920)(0.4920) * (0.2500 - 0.4920) = 0.2499 * -0.2420 = -0.0605 (rounded)
oGrad[1] = (1 - 0.5080)(0.5080) * (0.7500 - 0.5080) = 0.2499 * 0.2420 = 0.0605

The first part of the computation is the derivative term. The second part is the difference between computed and desired output values. The order in which the difference between computed and desired values is performed is very important but varies from implementation to implementation. Here, the difference is computed as (desired - computed) rather than (computed - desired).

Computing the values of the hidden node gradients uses the values of the output node gradients. The gradient of a hidden node is the derivative of its activation function times the sum of the products of "downstream" (to the right in **Figure 4-b**) output gradients and associated hidden-to-output weights. Note that computing gradient values in the way described here makes an implicit mathematical assumption about exactly how error is computed.

The calculation is best explained by example. As it turns out, the derivative of the hyperbolic tangent at some value y is $(1 - y)(1 + y)$. The gradient for hidden node 0, with rounding, is computed as:

hGrad[0]:
  derivative = (1 - 0.4699)(1 + 0.4699) = 0.5301 * 1.4699 = 0.7792
  sum = (-0.0605)(0.17) + (0.0605)(0.18) = -0.0103 + 0.0109 = 0.0006
  hGrad[0] = 0.7792 * 0.0006 = 0.00047 (rounded)

Similarly, the gradient for hidden node 1 is:

hGrad[1]:
  derivative = (1 - 0.5227)(1 + 0.5227) = 0.4773 * 1.5227 = 0.7268
  sum = (-0.0605)(0.19) + (0.0605)(0.20) = -0.0115 + 0.0121 = 0.0006
  hGrad[3] = 0.7268 * 0.0006 = 0.00044

And:

hGrad[2]:
  derivative = (1 - 0.5717)(1 + 0.5717) = 0.4283 * 1.5717= 0.6732
  sum = (-0.0605)(0.21) + (0.0605)(0.22) = -0.0127 + 0.0133 = 0.0006
  hGrad[3] = 0.6732 * 0.0006 = 0.00041

hGrad[3]:
  derivative = (1 - 0.6169)(1 + 0.6169) = 0.3831 * 1.6169 = 0.6194
  sum = (-0.0605)(0.23) + (0.0605)(0.24) = -0.0139 + 0.0145 = 0.0006
  hGrad[3] = 0.6194 * 0.0006 = 0.0037

Computing Weight and Bias Deltas

After all hidden node and output node gradient values have been computed, these values are used to compute a small delta value (which can be positive or negative) for each weight and bias. The delta value is added to the old weight or bias value. The new weights and bias values will, in theory, produce computed output values that are closer to the desired target output values.

The delta for a weight or bias is computed as the product of a small constant called the learning rate, the downstream (to the right) gradient, and the upstream (to the left) input value. Additionally, an extra value called the momentum factor is computed and added. The momentum factor is the product of a small constant called the momentum term, and the delta value from the previous iteration of the back-propagation algorithm.

As usual, the computation is best explained by example. Updating the weight from input node 0 to hidden node 0 is:

new ihWeight[0][0]:
  delta = 0.05 * 0.00047 * 1.0 = 0.000025
  ihWeight[0][0] = 0.01 + 0.000025 = 0.010025
  mFactor = 0.01 * 0.011 = 0.00011
  ihWeight[0][0] = 0.010025 + 0.00011 = 0.0101 (rounded)

The delta is 0.05 (the learning rate) times 0.00047 (the downstream gradient) times 1.0 (the upstream input). This delta, 0.000025, is added to the old weight value, 0.01, to give an updated weight value. Note that because the output node gradients were computed using (desired - computed) rather than (computed - desired), the delta value is added to the old weight value. If the output node gradients had been computed as (computed - desired) then delta values would be subtracted from the old weight values.

The momentum factor is 0.01 (the momentum term) times 0.011 (the previous delta). In the demo program, all previous delta values are arbitrarily set to 0.011 to initialize the algorithm. Initializing previous delta values is not necessary. If the initial previous delta values are all 0.0 then the momentum factor will be zero on the first iteration of the back-propagation algorithm, but will be (probably) non-zero from the second iteration onwards.

The computation of the new bias value for hidden node 0 is:

new hBias[0]:
  delta = 0.05 * 0.00047 = 0.000025
  hBias[0] = 0.13 + 0.000025 = 0.130025
  mFactor = 0.01 * 0.011 = 0.00011
  hBias[0] = 0.130025 + 0.00011 = 0.1301 (rounded)

The only difference between updating a weight and updating a bias is that bias values do not have any upstream input values. Another way of conceptualizing this is that bias values have dummy, constant 1.0 input values.

In **Figure 4-b**, updating the weight from hidden node 0 to output node 0 is:

new hoWeight[0][0]:
  delta = 0.05 * -0.0605 * 0.4699 = -0.001421
  hoWeight[0][0] = 0.17 + -0.001421= 0.168579
  mFactor = 0.01 * 0.011 = 0.00011
  hoWeight[0][0] = 0.168579 + 0.00011 = 0.1687 (rounded)

As before, the delta is the learning rate (0.05) times the downstream gradient (-0.0605) times the upstream input (0.4699).

Implementing the Back-Propagation Demo

To create the demo program I launched Visual Studio and created a new C# console application named BackProp. After the template code loaded into the editor, I removed all using statements except for the single statement referencing the top-level System namespace. The demo program has no significant .NET version dependencies, so any version of Visual Studio should work. In the Solution Explorer window, I renamed file Program.cs to BackPropProgram.cs and Visual Studio automatically renamed class Program to BackPropProgram.

The overall structure of the demo program is shown in **Listing 4-a**. The Main method in the program class has all the program logic. The program class houses two utility methods, ShowVector and ShowMatrix, which are useful for investigating the values in the inputs, biases, and outputs arrays, and in the input-to-hidden and hidden-to-output weights matrices.

The two display utilities are declared with public scope so that they can be placed and called from within methods in the NeuralNetwork class. Method ShowVector is defined:

```
public static void ShowVector(double[] vector, int valsPerRow, int decimals,
  bool newLine)
{
  for (int i = 0; i < vector.Length; ++i)
  {
    if (i > 0 && i % valsPerRow == 0)
      Console.WriteLine("");
    Console.Write(vector[i].ToString("F" + decimals).PadLeft(decimals + 4) + " ");
  }
  if (newLine == true) Console.WriteLine("");
}
```

```
using System;
namespace BackProp
{
  class BackPropProgram
  {
    static void Main(string[] args)
    {
      Console.WriteLine("\nBegin back-propagation demo\n");

      // All program control logic goes here.

      Console.WriteLine("\nEnd back-propagation demo\n");
      Console.ReadLine();
    }

    public static void ShowVector(double[] vector, int valsPerRow,
      int decimals,  bool newLine) { . . }
    public static void ShowMatrix(double[][] matrix, int decimals) { . . }
  } // Program

  public class NeuralNetwork
  {
    // Class fields go here.

    public NeuralNetwork(int numInput, int numHidden, int numOutput) { . . }
    public void SetWeights(double[] weights) { . . }
```

```
    public double[] GetWeights() { . . }
    public void FindWeights(double[] tValues, double[] xValues,
      double learnRate, double momentum, int maxEpochs) { . . }

    private static double[][] MakeMatrix(int rows, int cols) { . . }
    private static void InitMatrix(double[][] matrix, double value) { . . }
    private static void InitVector(double[] vector, double value) { . . }
    private double[] ComputeOutputs(double[] xValues) { . . }
    private static double HyperTan(double v) { . . }
    private static double[] Softmax(double[] oSums) { . . }
    private void UpdateWeights(double[] tValues, double learnRate, double momentum) { . . }
  }
} // ns
```

Listing 4-a: Back-Prop Demo Program Structure

Utility method ShowMatrix takes advantage of the fact that the demo uses an array-of-arrays style matrix and calls method ShowVector on each row array of its matrix parameter:

```
public static void ShowMatrix(double[][] matrix, int decimals)
{
  int cols = matrix[0].Length;
  for (int i = 0; i < matrix.Length; ++i) // Each row.
    ShowVector(matrix[i], cols, decimals, true);
}
```

The Main method begins by instantiating a dummy 3-4-2 neural network:

```
static void Main(string[] args)
{
  Console.WriteLine("\nBegin back-propagation demo\n");
  Console.WriteLine("Creating a 3-4-2 neural network\n");
  int numInput = 3;
  int numHidden = 4;
  int numOutput = 2;
  NeuralNetwork nn = new NeuralNetwork(numInput, numHidden, numOutput);
```

Because the number of input, hidden, and output nodes does not change, you might want to consider making these values constants rather than variables. Notice that there is nothing in the constructor call to indicate that the neural network uses back-propagation. You might want to wrap the main logic code in try-catch blocks to handle exceptions.

Next, the demo program initializes the neural network's weights and bias values:

```
double[] weights = new double[26] {
  0.01, 0.02, 0.03, 0.04, 0.05, 0.06, 0.07, 0.08,
  0.09, 0.10, 0.11, 0.12, 0.13, 0.14, 0.15, 0.16,
  0.17, 0.18, 0.19, 0.20, 0.21, 0.22, 0.23, 0.24,
  0.25, 0.26 };
Console.WriteLine("Setting dummy initial weights to:");
ShowVector(weights, 8, 2, true);
nn.SetWeights(weights);
```

The initial weights and bias values are sequential from 0.01 to 0.26 only to make the explanation of the back-propagation algorithm easier to visualize. In a non-demo scenario, neural network weights and bias values would typically be set to small random values.

Next, the demo sets up fixed input values and desired target output values:

```
double[] xValues = new double[3] { 1.0, 2.0, 3.0 }; // Inputs.
double[] tValues = new double[2] { 0.2500, 0.7500 }; // Target outputs.
Console.WriteLine("\nSetting fixed inputs = ");
ShowVector(xValues, 3, 1, true);
Console.WriteLine("Setting fixed target outputs = ");
ShowVector(tValues, 2, 4, true);
```

In the demo there is just a single input and corresponding target item. In a realistic neural network training scenario, there would be many input items, each with its own target values.

Next, the demo program prepares to use the back-propagation algorithm by setting the values of the parameters:

```
double learnRate = 0.05;
double momentum = 0.01;
int maxEpochs = 1000;
Console.WriteLine("\nSetting learning rate = " + learnRate.ToString("F2"));
Console.WriteLine("Setting momentum = " + momentum.ToString("F2"));
Console.WriteLine("Setting max epochs = " + maxEpochs + "\n");
```

If you review the back-propagation algorithm explanation in the previous sections of this chapter, you'll see that the learning rate affects the magnitude of the delta value to be added to a weight or bias. Larger values of the learning rate create larger delta values, which in turn adjust weights and biases faster. So why not just use a very large learning rate, for example with value 1.0? Large values of the learning rate run the risk of adjusting weights and bias values too much at each iteration of the back-propagation algorithm. This could lead to a situation where weights and bias values continuously overshoot, and then undershoot, optimal values.

On the other hand, a very small learning rate value usually leads to slow but steady improvement in a neural network's weights and bias values. However, if the learning rate is too small then training time can be unacceptably long. Practice suggests that as a general rule of thumb it's better to use smaller values for the learning rate—larger values tend to lead to poor results quite frequently.

Early implementations of back-propagation did not use a momentum term. Momentum is an additional factor added (or essentially subtracted if the factor is negative) to each weight and bias value. The use of momentum is primarily designed to speed up training when the learning rate is small, as it usually is. Notice that by setting the value of the momentum term to 0.0, you will essentially omit the momentum factor.

Finding good values for the learning rate and the momentum term is mostly a matter of trial and error. The back-propagation algorithm tends to be very sensitive to the values selected, meaning that even a small change in learning rate or momentum can lead to a very big change, either good or bad, in the behavior of the algorithm.

The maxEpochs value of 1,000 is a loop count limit. The value was determined by trial and error for the demo program, which was possible only because it was easy to see when computed output values were very close to the desired output values. In a non-demo scenario, the back-propagation loop is often terminated when some measure of error between computed outputs and desired outputs drops below some threshold value.

The demo program concludes by calling the public method that uses the back-propagation algorithm:

```
nn.FindWeights(tValues, xValues, learnRate, momentum, maxEpochs);
double[] bestWeights = nn.GetWeights();
Console.WriteLine("\nBest weights found:");
ShowVector(bestWeights, 8, 4, true);
Console.WriteLine("\nEnd back-propagation demo\n");
Console.ReadLine();
} // Main
```

The calling method is named FindWeights rather than something like Train to emphasize the fact that the method is intended to illustrate the back-propagation algorithm, as opposed to actually training the neural network which requires more than a single set of input and target values.

The Neural Network Class Definition

The design of a neural network class which supports back-propagation requires several additional fields in addition to the fields needed for the feed-forward mechanism that computes output values. The structure of the demo neural network is presented in **Listing 4-b**.

```
public class NeuralNetwork
{
  private int numInput;
  private int numHidden;
  private int numOutput;

  private double[] inputs;

  private double[][] ihWeights;
  private double[] hBiases;
  private double[] hOutputs;

  private double[][] hoWeights;
  private double[] oBiases;
  private double[] outputs;

  private double[] oGrads; // Output gradients for back-propagation.
  private double[] hGrads; // Hidden gradients for back-propagation.
```

```
private double[][] ihPrevWeightsDelta;    // For momentum with back-propagation.
private double[] hPrevBiasesDelta;
private double[][] hoPrevWeightsDelta;
private double[] oPrevBiasesDelta;

// Constructor and methods go here.
}
```

Listing 4-b: Demo Neural Network Member Fields

The demo neural network has six arrays that are used by the back-propagation algorithm. Recall that back-propagation computes a gradient for each output and hidden node. Arrays oGrads and hGrads hold the values of the output node gradients and the hidden node gradients respectively. Also, recall that for each weight and bias, the momentum factor is the product of the momentum term (0.01 in the demo) and the value of the previous delta from the last iteration for the weight or bias. Matrix ihPrevWeightsDelta holds the values of the previous deltas for the input-to-hidden weights. Similarly, matrix hoPrevWeightsDelta holds the previous delta values for the hidden-to-output weights. Arrays hPrevBiasesDelta and oPrevBiasesDelta hold the previous delta values for the hidden node biases and the output node biases respectively.

At first thought, it might seem that placing the six arrays and matrices related to back-propagation inside the method that performs back-propagation would be a cleaner design. However, because in almost all implementations these arrays and matrices are needed by more than one class method, placing the arrays and matrices as in **Listing 4-b** is more efficient.

The Neural Network Constructor

The code for the neural network constructor is presented in **Listing 4-c**. The constructor accepts parameters for the number of input, hidden, and output nodes. The activation functions are hardwired into the neural network's definition. An alternative is to pass two additional parameter values to the constructor to indicate what activation functions to use.

```
public NeuralNetwork(int numInput, int numHidden, int numOutput)
{
  this.numInput = numInput;
  this.numHidden = numHidden;
  this.numOutput = numOutput;

  this.inputs = new double[numInput];
  this.ihWeights = MakeMatrix(numInput, numHidden);
  this.hBiases = new double[numHidden];
  this.hOutputs = new double[numHidden];

  this.hoWeights = MakeMatrix(numHidden, numOutput);
  this.oBiases = new double[numOutput];
  this.outputs = new double[numOutput];

  oGrads = new double[numOutput];
  hGrads = new double[numHidden];

  ihPrevWeightsDelta = MakeMatrix(numInput, numHidden);
  hPrevBiasesDelta = new double[numHidden];
  hoPrevWeightsDelta = MakeMatrix(numHidden, numOutput);
```

```
    oPrevBiasesDelta = new double[numOutput];

    InitMatrix(ihPrevWeightsDelta, 0.011);
    InitVector(hPrevBiasesDelta, 0.011);
    InitMatrix(hoPrevWeightsDelta, 0.011);
    InitVector(oPrevBiasesDelta, 0.011);
}
```

Listing 4-c: The Constructor

The first few lines of the constructor are exactly the same as those used for the demo feed-forward neural network in the previous chapter. The input-to-hidden weights matrix and the hidden-to-output weights matrix are allocated using private helper method MakeMatrix:

```
private static double[][] MakeMatrix(int rows, int cols)
{
  double[][] result = new double[rows][];
  for (int i = 0; i < rows; ++i)
    result[i] = new double[cols];
  return result;
}
```

Each input-to-hidden and hidden-to-output node requires a previous delta, and method MakeMatrix is used to allocate space for those two matrices too. The arrays for the output node and hidden node gradients, and the arrays for the previous deltas for the hidden node biases and output node biases, are allocated directly using the "new" keyword.

The constructor calls two private static utility methods, InitMatrix and InitVector, to initialize all previous delta values to 0.011. As explained earlier, this is not necessary and is done to make the back-propagation explanation in the previous sections easier to understand.

Method InitVector is defined as:

```
private static void InitVector(double[] vector, double value)
{
  for (int i = 0; i < vector.Length; ++i)
    vector[i] = value;
}
```

And method InitMatrix is defined as:

```
private static void InitMatrix(double[][] matrix, double value)
{
  int rows = matrix.Length;
  int cols = matrix[0].Length;
  for (int i = 0; i < rows; ++i)
    for (int j = 0; j < cols; ++j)
      matrix[i][j] = value;
}
```

Notice that the constructor uses static methods InitVector and InitMatrix to initialize all previous weights and bias values. An alternative approach would be to write a non-static class method InitializeAllPrev that accepts a value of type double, and then iterates through the four previous-delta arrays and matrices, initializing them to the parameter value.

Getting and Setting Weights and Biases

The demo program uses class methods SetWeights and GetWeights to assign and retrieve the values of the neural network's weights and biases. The code for SetWeights and GetWeights is presented in **Listings 4-d** and **4-e**.

```
public void SetWeights(double[] weights)
{
    int k = 0; // Pointer into weights parameter.

    for (int i = 0; i < numInput; ++i)
      for (int j = 0; j < numHidden; ++j)
        ihWeights[i][j] = weights[k++];

    for (int i = 0; i < numHidden; ++i)
      hBiases[i] = weights[k++];

    for (int i = 0; i < numHidden; ++i)
      for (int j = 0; j < numOutput; ++j)
        hoWeights[i][j] = weights[k++];

    for (int i = 0; i < numOutput; ++i)
      oBiases[i] = weights[k++];
}
```

Listing 4-d: Setting Weights and Bias Values

Method SetWeights accepts an array parameter that holds all weights and bias values. The order in which the values are stored is assumed to be (1) input-to-hidden weights, (2) hidden node biases, (3) hidden-to-output weights, and (4) output biases. The weights values are assumed to be stored in row-major form; in other words, the values are transferred from the array into the two weights matrices from left to right and top to bottom.

You might want to consider doing an input parameter error-check inside SetWeights:

```
int numWeights = (numInput * numHidden) + numHidden +
  (numHidden * numOutput) + numOutput;
if (weights.Length != numWeights)
  throw new Exception("Bad weights array length in SetWeights");
```

An alternative approach for method SetWeights is to refactor or overload the method to accept four parameters along the lines of:

```
public void SetWeights(double[][] ihWeights, double[] hBiases,
  double[][] hoWeights, double[] oBiases)
```

Method GetWeights is symmetric to SetWeights. The return value is an array where the values are the input-to-hidden weights (in row-major form), followed by the hidden biases, followed by the hidden-to-output weights, followed by the output biases.

```
public double[] GetWeights()
{
    int numWeights = (numInput * numHidden) + numHidden + (numHidden * numOutput) + numOutput;
```

```
double[] result = new double[numWeights];
int k = 0;  // Pointer into results array.

for (int i = 0; i < numInput; ++i)
  for (int j = 0; j < numHidden; ++j)
    result[k++] = ihWeights[i][j];

for (int i = 0; i < numHidden; ++i)
  result[k++] = hBiases[i];

for (int i = 0; i < numHidden; ++i)
  for (int j = 0; j < numOutput; ++j)
    result[k++] = hoWeights[i][j];

for (int i = 0; i < numOutput; ++i)
  result[k++] = oBiases[i];

return result;
}
```

Listing 4-e: Getting Weights and Bias Values

Unlike method SetWeights, which can be easily refactored to accept separate weights and bias arrays, it would be a bit awkward to refactor method GetWeights to return separate arrays. One approach would be to use out-parameters. Another approach would be to define a weights and bias values container class or structure.

Computing Output Values

Back-propagation compares computed output values with desired output values to compute gradients, which in turn are used to compute deltas, which in turn are used to modify weights and bias values. Class method ComputeOutputs is presented in **Listing 4-f**.

```
private double[] ComputeOutputs(double[] xValues)
{
  double[] hSums = new double[numHidden];
  double[] oSums = new double[numOutput];

  for (int i = 0; i < xValues.Length; ++i)
    inputs[i] = xValues[i];

  for (int j = 0; j < numHidden; ++j)
    for (int i = 0; i < numInput; ++i)
      hSums[j] += inputs[i] * ihWeights[i][j];

  for (int i = 0; i < numHidden; ++i)
    hSums[i] += hBiases[i];

  for (int i = 0; i < numHidden; ++i)
    hOutputs[i] = HyperTan(hSums[i]);

  for (int j = 0; j < numOutput; ++j)
    for (int i = 0; i < numHidden; ++i)
      oSums[j] += hOutputs[i] * hoWeights[i][j];
```

```
  for (int i = 0; i < numOutput; ++i)
    oSums[i] += oBiases[i];

  double[] softOut = Softmax(oSums); // Softmax does all outputs at once.
  for (int i = 0; i < outputs.Length; ++i)
    outputs[i] = softOut[i];

  double[] result = new double[numOutput];
  for (int i = 0; i < outputs.Length; ++i)
    result[i] = outputs[i];

  return result;
}
```

Listing 4-f: Computing Output Values

Method ComputeOutputs implements the normal feed-forward mechanism for a fully connected neural network. When working with neural networks there is often a tradeoff between error-checking and performance. For example, in method ComputeOutputs, you might consider adding an input parameter check like:

```
if (xValues.Length != this.numInput)
  throw new Exception("Bad xValues array length in ComputeOutputs");
```

However, in a non-demo scenario, method ComputeOutputs will typically be called many thousands of times during training and such error checking can have a big negative effect on performance. One possible strategy is to initially include error checking during development and then slowly remove the checks over time as you become more confident in the correctness of your code.

The hardwired hidden layer hyperbolic tangent activation function is defined as:

```
private static double HyperTan(double v)
{
  if (v < -20.0)
    return -1.0;
  else if (v > 20.0)
    return 1.0;
  else
    return Math.Tanh(v);
}
```

The hardwired output layer softmax activation function is presented in **Listing 4-g**. Recall the important relationship between activation functions and back-propagation. When computing output node and hidden node gradient values, it is necessary to use the calculus derivative of the output layer and hidden layer activation functions.

```
private static double[] Softmax(double[] oSums)
{
  double max = oSums[0];
  for (int i = 0; i < oSums.Length; ++i)
    if (oSums[i] > max)
      max = oSums[i];

  double scale = 0.0;
```

```
  for (int i = 0; i < oSums.Length; ++i)
    scale += Math.Exp(oSums[i] - max);

  double[] result = new double[oSums.Length];
  for (int i = 0; i < oSums.Length; ++i)
    result[i] = Math.Exp(oSums[i] - max) / scale;

  return result; // xi sum to 1.0.
}
```

Listing 4-g: Softmax Activation

In practical terms, except in rare situations, there are just three activation functions commonly used in neural networks: the hyperbolic tangent function, the logistic sigmoid function, and the softmax function. The calculus derivatives of these three functions at some value y are:

hyperbolic tangent: $(1 - y)(1 + y)$
logistic sigmoid: $y(1 - y)$
softmax: $y(1 - y)$

Notice the derivatives of the logistic sigmoid and softmax activations functions are the same. The mathematical explanation of exactly why calculus derivatives of the activation functions are needed to compute gradients is fascinating (if you like mathematics) but are outside the scope of this book.

Implementing the FindWeights Method

The demo program implements back-propagation in public class method FindWeights. The code for FindWeights is presented in **Listing 4-h**.

If you examine method FindWeights you'll quickly see that the method is really a wrapper that iteratively calls private methods ComputeOutputs and UpdateWeights. In some implementations, method ComputeOutputs is called FeedForward and method UpdateWeights is called BackPropagation. Using this terminology, the pseudo-code would resemble:

```
loop until some exit condition is met
  FeedForward
  BackPropagation
end loop
```

However, this terminology can be somewhat ambiguous because back-propagation would then refer to the overall process of updating weights and also a specific back-propagation method in the implementation.

```
public void FindWeights(double[] tValues, double[] xValues, double learnRate,
    double momentum, int maxEpochs)
{
  int epoch = 0;
  while (epoch <= maxEpochs)
  {
    double[] yValues = ComputeOutputs(xValues);
    UpdateWeights(tValues, learnRate, momentum);
```

```
if (epoch % 100 == 0)
{
  Console.Write("epoch = " + epoch.ToString().PadLeft(5) + "   curr outputs = ");
  BackPropProgram.ShowVector(yValues, 2, 4, true);
}

++epoch;
} // Find loop.
}
```

Listing 4-h: Finding Weights and Bias Values so Computed Outputs Match Target Outputs

Method FindWeights accepts five input parameter values. Array parameter tValues holds the desired target values. An error check on tValues could verify that the length of the array is the same as the value in class member variable numOutput. Array parameter xValues holds the input values to be fed into the neural network. An error check on xValues could verify that the length of xValues is the same as class member variable numInput.

Parameter learnRate holds the learning rate value. Although the concept of the learning rate is standard in neural network research and practice, there are variations across different implementations in exactly how the learning rate value is used. So, a learning rate value that works well for a particular problem in a particular neural network implementation might not work at all for the same problem but using a different neural network implementation.

Parameter momentum holds the momentum term value. Strictly speaking, the use of a momentum term is independent of the back-propagation algorithm, but in practice momentum is used more often than not. As with the learning rate, momentum can be implemented in different ways so for a given problem, a good momentum value on one system may not be a good value on some other system.

Parameter maxEpochs sets the number of times the compute-outputs and update-weights loop iterates. Because variable epochs is initialized to 0 and the loop condition is less-than-or-equal-to rather than less-than, the loop actually iterates maxEpochs + 1 times. A common alternative to using a fixed number of iterations is to iterate until there is no change, or a very small change, in the weights and bias values. Note that when momentum is used, this information is available in the previous-delta arrays and matrices.

Method FindWeights displays the current neural network output values every 100 iterations. Notice that static helper method ShowVector is public to the main BackPropProgram class and so is visible to class NeuralNetwork when the method is qualified by the class name. The ability to insert diagnostic output anywhere is a big advantage of writing custom neural network code, compared to the alternative of using a canned system where you don't have access to source code.

Implementing the Back-Propagation Algorithm

The heart of the back-propagation algorithm is implemented in method UpdateWeights. The definition of method UpdateWeights begins as:

```
private void UpdateWeights(double[] tValues, double learnRate, double momentum)
{
  if (tValues.Length != numOutput)
    throw new Exception("target array not same length as output in UpdateWeights");
```

The method is declared with private scope because it is used in method FindWeights which is exposed to the calling program. During development you will likely find it useful to declare UpdateWeights as public so that it can be tested directly from a test harness. Method UpdateWeights accepts three parameters. Notice that because UpdateWeights is a class member it has direct access to the class outputs array and so the current output values do not have to be passed in as an array parameter to the method. Method UpdateWeights performs a preliminary error check of the length of the target values array. In a non-demo scenario you would most often omit this check in order to improve performance.

The method continues by computing the gradients of each of the output layer nodes:

```
for (int i = 0; i < oGrads.Length; ++i)
{
  double derivative = (1 - outputs[i]) * outputs[i];
  oGrads[i] = derivative * (tValues[i] - outputs[i]);
}
```

Recall that because the demo neural network uses softmax activation, the calculus derivative at value y is $y(1 - y)$. Also note that the demo implementation uses (target - computed) rather than (computed - target). The order in which target output values and computed output values are subtracted is something you must watch for very carefully when comparing different neural network implementations.

Because UpdateWeights accesses the class array outputs, there is what might be called a synchronization dependency. In other words, method UpdateWeights assumes that method ComputeOutputs has been called so that the outputs array holds the currently computed output values.

Next, method UpdateWeights computes the gradients for each hidden layer node:

```
for (int i = 0; i < hGrads.Length; ++i)
{
  double derivative = (1 - hOutputs[i]) * (1 + hOutputs[i]);
  double sum = 0.0;
  for (int j = 0; j < numOutput; ++j)
    sum += oGrads[j] * hoWeights[i][j];
  hGrads[i] = derivative * sum;
}
```

As explained earlier, the demo uses the hyperbolic tangent function for hidden layer activation, and the derivative of the hyperbolic tangent at value y is $(1 - y)(1 + y)$. Although short, these few lines of code are quite tricky. The local variable "sum" accumulates the product of each downstream gradient (the output node gradients) and its associated hidden-to-output weight.

Next, UpdateWeights adjusts the input-to-hidden weights:

```
for (int i = 0; i < ihWeights.Length; ++i)
{
```

```
  for (int j = 0; j < ihWeights[i].Length; ++j)
  {
    double delta = learnRate * hGrads[j] * inputs[i];
    ihWeights[i][j] += delta;
    ihWeights[i][j] += momentum * ihPrevWeightsDelta[i][j];
    ihPrevWeightsDelta[i][j] = delta; // Save the delta.
  }
}
```

Again, the code is short but the logic is quite subtle. There are some fascinating low-level coding details involved too. The nested for-loops iterate through the input-to-hidden weights matrix using a standard approach. There are several alternatives. One alternative is to use the fact that all the columns of the matrix have the same length and just use the length of the first row like so:

```
for (int i = 0; i < ihWeights.Length; ++i)
{
  for (int j = 0; j < ihWeights[0].Length; ++j)
```

Another alternative is to recall that the input-to-hidden weights matrix has a number of rows equal to the neural network's number of input values. And the matrix has a number of columns equal to the number of hidden nodes. Therefore you could code it as:

```
for (int i = 0; i < this.numInput; ++i)
{
  for (int j = 0; j < this.numHidden; ++j)
```

An examination of the intermediate language generated by each approach shows that using numInput and numHidden is shorter by five intermediate language instructions. This comes at the expense of a slight loss of clarity.

Method UpdateWeights continues by updating the hidden node biases:

```
for (int i = 0; i < hBiases.Length; ++i)
{
  double delta = learnRate * hGrads[i];
  hBiases[i] += delta;
  hBiases[i] += momentum * hPrevBiasesDelta[i];
  hPrevBiasesDelta[i] = delta; // Save delta.
}
```

Because biases can be considered special weights that have dummy constant 1.0 value inputs, some implementations of the back-propagation compute delta as:

```
double delta = learnRate * hGrads[i] * 1.0;
```

This involves an unneeded multiplication operation but makes the computation of the delta for a bias value symmetric with the computation of the delta for a normal weight value.

Next, the method updates the hidden-to-output weights:

```
for (int i = 0; i < hoWeights.Length; ++i)
{
```

```
    for (int j = 0; j < hoWeights[i].Length; ++j)
    {
      double delta = learnRate * oGrads[j] * hOutputs[i];
      hoWeights[i][j] += delta;
      hoWeights[i][j] += momentum * hoPrevWeightsDelta[i][j];
      hoPrevWeightsDelta[i][j] = delta; // Save delta.
    }
  }
}
```

Method UpdateWeights finishes by updating the output node biases:

```
  for (int i = 0; i < oBiases.Length; ++i)
  {
    double delta = learnRate * oGrads[i] * 1.0;
    oBiases[i] += delta;
    oBiases[i] += momentum * oPrevBiasesDelta[i];
    oPrevBiasesDelta[i] = delta; // Save delta.
  }
} // UpdateWeights
```

The last four blocks of code which update weights and biases—the input-to-hidden weights, the hidden node biases, the hidden-to-output weights, and the output node biases—can be performed in any order.

Complete Demo Program Source Code

```
using System;
namespace BackProp
{
  class BackPropProgram
  {
    static void Main(string[] args)
    {
      Console.WriteLine("\nBegin back-propagation demo\n");

      Console.WriteLine("Creating a 3-4-2 neural network\n");
      int numInput = 3;
      int numHidden = 4;
      int numOutput = 2;
      NeuralNetwork nn = new NeuralNetwork(numInput, numHidden, numOutput);

      double[] weights = new double[26] {
          0.01, 0.02, 0.03, 0.04, 0.05, 0.06, 0.07, 0.08,
          0.09, 0.10, 0.11, 0.12, 0.13, 0.14, 0.15, 0.16,
          0.17, 0.18, 0.19, 0.20, 0.21, 0.22, 0.23, 0.24,
          0.25, 0.26 };

      Console.WriteLine("Setting dummy initial weights to:");
      ShowVector(weights, 8, 2, true);
      nn.SetWeights(weights);

      double[] xValues = new double[3] { 1.0, 2.0, 3.0 }; // Inputs.
      double[] tValues = new double[2] { 0.2500, 0.7500 }; // Target outputs.
```

```
        Console.WriteLine("\nSetting fixed inputs = ");
        ShowVector(xValues, 3, 1, true);
        Console.WriteLine("Setting fixed target outputs = ");
        ShowVector(tValues, 2, 4, true);


        double learnRate = 0.05;
        double momentum = 0.01;
        int maxEpochs = 1000;
        Console.WriteLine("\nSetting learning rate = " + learnRate.ToString("F2"));
        Console.WriteLine("Setting momentum = " + momentum.ToString("F2"));
        Console.WriteLine("Setting max epochs = " + maxEpochs + "\n");

        nn.FindWeights(tValues, xValues, learnRate, momentum, maxEpochs);

        double[] bestWeights = nn.GetWeights();
        Console.WriteLine("\nBest weights found:");
        ShowVector(bestWeights, 8, 4, true);

        Console.WriteLine("\nEnd back-propagation demo\n");
        Console.ReadLine();
      } // Main

    public static void ShowVector(double[] vector, int valsPerRow, int decimals, bool
newLine)
      {
        for (int i = 0; i < vector.Length; ++i)
        {
          if (i > 0 && i % valsPerRow == 0)
            Console.WriteLine("");
          Console.Write(vector[i].ToString("F" + decimals).PadLeft(decimals + 4) + " ");
        }

        if (newLine == true) Console.WriteLine("");
      }

    public static void ShowMatrix(double[][] matrix, int decimals)
      {
        int cols = matrix[0].Length;
        for (int i = 0; i < matrix.Length; ++i) // Each row.
          ShowVector(matrix[i], cols, decimals, true);
      }
    } // Program class

    public class NeuralNetwork
    {
      private int numInput;
      private int numHidden;
      private int numOutput;

      private double[] inputs;

      private double[][] ihWeights;
      private double[] hBiases;
      private double[] hOutputs;

      private double[][] hoWeights;
      private double[] oBiases;
      private double[] outputs;

      private double[] oGrads; // Output gradients for back-propagation.
```

```
private double[] hGrads; // Hidden gradients for back-propagation.

private double[][] ihPrevWeightsDelta;   // For momentum.
private double[] hPrevBiasesDelta;
private double[][] hoPrevWeightsDelta;
private double[] oPrevBiasesDelta;

public NeuralNetwork(int numInput, int numHidden, int numOutput)
{
  this.numInput = numInput;
  this.numHidden = numHidden;
  this.numOutput = numOutput;

  this.inputs = new double[numInput];
  this.ihWeights = MakeMatrix(numInput, numHidden);
  this.hBiases = new double[numHidden];
  this.hOutputs = new double[numHidden];

  this.hoWeights = MakeMatrix(numHidden, numOutput);
  this.oBiases = new double[numOutput];
  this.outputs = new double[numOutput];

  oGrads = new double[numOutput];
  hGrads = new double[numHidden];

  ihPrevWeightsDelta = MakeMatrix(numInput, numHidden);
  hPrevBiasesDelta = new double[numHidden];
  hoPrevWeightsDelta = MakeMatrix(numHidden, numOutput);
  oPrevBiasesDelta = new double[numOutput];

  InitMatrix(ihPrevWeightsDelta, 0.011);
  InitVector(hPrevBiasesDelta, 0.011);
  InitMatrix(hoPrevWeightsDelta, 0.011);
  InitVector(oPrevBiasesDelta, 0.011);
}

private static double[][] MakeMatrix(int rows, int cols)
{
  double[][] result = new double[rows][];
  for (int i = 0; i < rows; ++i)
    result[i] = new double[cols];
  return result;
}

private static void InitMatrix(double[][] matrix, double value)
{
  int rows = matrix.Length;
  int cols = matrix[0].Length;
  for (int i = 0; i < rows; ++i)
    for (int j = 0; j < cols; ++j)
      matrix[i][j] = value;
}

private static void InitVector(double[] vector, double value)
{
  for (int i = 0; i < vector.Length; ++i)
    vector[i] = value;
}

public void SetWeights(double[] weights)
{
```

```
//int numWeights = (numInput * numHidden) + numHidden +
// (numHidden * numOutput) + numOutput;
//if (weights.Length != numWeights)
// throw new Exception("Bad weights array");

int k = 0; // Pointer into weights.

for (int i = 0; i < numInput; ++i)
  for (int j = 0; j < numHidden; ++j)
    ihWeights[i][j] = weights[k++];

for (int i = 0; i < numHidden; ++i)
  hBiases[i] = weights[k++];

for (int i = 0; i < numHidden; ++i)
  for (int j = 0; j < numOutput; ++j)
    hoWeights[i][j] = weights[k++];

for (int i = 0; i < numOutput; ++i)
  oBiases[i] = weights[k++];
}

public double[] GetWeights()
{
  int numWeights = (numInput * numHidden) + numHidden +
    (numHidden * numOutput) + numOutput;
  double[] result = new double[numWeights];

  int k = 0;
  for (int i = 0; i < numInput; ++i)
    for (int j = 0; j < numHidden; ++j)
      result[k++] = ihWeights[i][j];

  for (int i = 0; i < numHidden; ++i)
    result[k++] = hBiases[i];

  for (int i = 0; i < numHidden; ++i)
    for (int j = 0; j < numOutput; ++j)
      result[k++] = hoWeights[i][j];

  for (int i = 0; i < numOutput; ++i)
    result[k++] = oBiases[i];

  return result;
}

private double[] ComputeOutputs(double[] xValues)
{
  if (xValues.Length != numInput)
    throw new Exception("Bad xValues array");

  double[] hSums = new double[numHidden];
  double[] oSums = new double[numOutput];

  for (int i = 0; i < xValues.Length; ++i)
    inputs[i] = xValues[i];

  for (int j = 0; j < numHidden; ++j)
    for (int i = 0; i < numInput; ++i)
      hSums[j] += inputs[i] * ihWeights[i][j];
```

```
    for (int i = 0; i < numHidden; ++i)
      hSums[i] += hBiases[i];

    for (int i = 0; i < numHidden; ++i)
      hOutputs[i] = HyperTan(hSums[i]);

    for (int j = 0; j < numOutput; ++j)
      for (int i = 0; i < numHidden; ++i)
        oSums[j] += hOutputs[i] * hoWeights[i][j];

    for (int i = 0; i < numOutput; ++i)
      oSums[i] += oBiases[i];

    double[] softOut = Softmax(oSums); // All outputs at once.
    for (int i = 0; i < outputs.Length; ++i)
      outputs[i] = softOut[i];

    double[] result = new double[numOutput];
    for (int i = 0; i < outputs.Length; ++i)
      result[i] = outputs[i];

    return result;
}

private static double HyperTan(double v)
{
  if (v < -20.0)
    return -1.0;
  else if (v > 20.0)
    return 1.0;
  else  return Math.Tanh(v);
}

private static double[] Softmax(double[] oSums)
{
  double max = oSums[0];
  for (int i = 0; i < oSums.Length; ++i)
    if (oSums[i] > max)
      max = oSums[i];

  double scale = 0.0;
  for (int i = 0; i < oSums.Length; ++i)
    scale += Math.Exp(oSums[i] - max);

  double[] result = new double[oSums.Length];
  for (int i = 0; i < oSums.Length; ++i)
    result[i] = Math.Exp(oSums[i] - max) / scale;

  return result; // xi sum to 1.0.
}

public void FindWeights(double[] tValues, double[] xValues, double learnRate,
  double momentum, int maxEpochs)
{
  // Call UpdateWeights maxEpoch times.
  int epoch = 0;
  while (epoch <= maxEpochs)
  {
    double[] yValues = ComputeOutputs(xValues);
    UpdateWeights(tValues, learnRate, momentum);
```

```
      if (epoch % 100 == 0)
      {
        Console.Write("epoch = " + epoch.ToString().PadLeft(5) + "   curr outputs = ");
        BackPropProgram.ShowVector(yValues, 2, 4, true);
      }

      ++epoch;
    } // Find loop.
  }

  private void UpdateWeights(double[] tValues, double learnRate, double momentum)
  {
    // Assumes that SetWeights and ComputeOutputs have been called.
    if (tValues.Length != numOutput)
      throw new Exception("target values not same Length as output in UpdateWeights");

    // 1. Compute output gradients. Assumes softmax.
    for (int i = 0; i < oGrads.Length; ++i)
    {
      double derivative = (1 - outputs[i]) * outputs[i]; // Derivative of softmax is y(1-
y).
      oGrads[i] = derivative * (tValues[i] - outputs[i]); // oGrad = (1 - 0)(0) * (T-O)
    }

    // 2. Compute hidden gradients. Assumes tanh!
    for (int i = 0; i < hGrads.Length; ++i)
    {
      double derivative = (1 - hOutputs[i]) * (1 + hOutputs[i]); // f' of tanh is (1-
y)(1+y).
      double sum = 0.0;
      for (int j = 0; j < numOutput; ++j) // Each hidden delta is the sum of numOutput
terms.
        sum += oGrads[j] * hoWeights[i][j]; // Each downstream gradient * outgoing weight.
      hGrads[i] = derivative * sum; // hGrad = (1-0)(1+0) * Sum(oGrads*oWts)
    }

    // 3. Update input to hidden weights.
    for (int i = 0; i < ihWeights.Length; ++i)
    {
      for (int j = 0; j < ihWeights[i].Length; ++j)
      {
        double delta = learnRate * hGrads[j] * inputs[i];
        ihWeights[i][j] += delta; // Update.
        ihWeights[i][j] += momentum * ihPrevWeightsDelta[i][j]; // Add momentum factor.
        ihPrevWeightsDelta[i][j] = delta; // Save the delta for next time.
      }
    }

    // 4. Update hidden biases.
    for (int i = 0; i < hBiases.Length; ++i)
    {
      double delta = learnRate * hGrads[i] * 1.0; // The 1.0 is a dummy value; it could be
left out.
      hBiases[i] += delta;
      hBiases[i] += momentum * hPrevBiasesDelta[i];
      hPrevBiasesDelta[i] = delta; // Save delta.
    }

    // 5. Update hidden to output weights.
    for (int i = 0; i < hoWeights.Length; ++i)
    {
```

```
      for (int j = 0; j < hoWeights[i].Length; ++j)
      {
        double delta = learnRate * oGrads[j] * hOutputs[i];
        hoWeights[i][j] += delta;
        hoWeights[i][j] += momentum * hoPrevWeightsDelta[i][j];
        hoPrevWeightsDelta[i][j] = delta; // Save delta.
      }
    }

    // 6. Update output biases.
    for (int i = 0; i < oBiases.Length; ++i)
    {
      double delta = learnRate * oGrads[i] * 1.0;
      oBiases[i] += delta;
      oBiases[i] += momentum * oPrevBiasesDelta[i];
      oPrevBiasesDelta[i] = delta; // Save delta.
    }
  } // UpdateWeights
 } // NN class
} // ns
```

Chapter 5 Training

Introduction

The ultimate goal of a neural network is to make a prediction. In order to make a prediction, a neural network must first be trained. Training a neural network is the process of finding a set of good weights and bias values so that the known outputs of some training data match the outputs computed using the weights and bias values. The resulting weights and bias values for a particular problem are often collectively called a model. The model can then be used to predict the output for previously unseen inputs that do not have known output values.

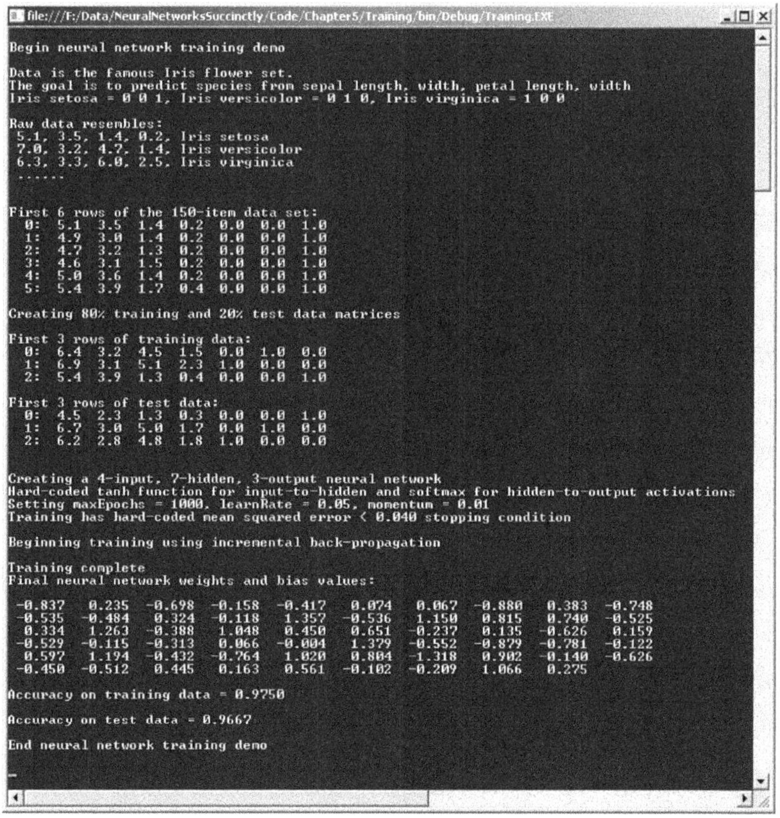

Figure 5-a: Training Demo

To get a good feel for exactly what neural network training is, take a look at the screenshot of a demo program in **Figure 5-a**. The demo program solves a simple, but what is probably the most famous, problem in the field of neural networks. The goal is to predict the species of an iris flower from four numeric attributes of the flower: petal length, petal width, sepal length, and sepal width. The petal is what most people would consider the actual flower part of the iris. The sepal is a green structure that you can think of as a specialized leaf. There are three possible species: *Iris setosa*, *Iris versicolor*, and *Iris virginica*. The data set was first published in 1936 by mathematician Ronald Fisher and so it is often called Fisher's Iris data.

The data set consists of a total of 150 items, with data for 50 of each of the three species of iris. Because neural networks only understand numeric data, the demo must use data where the three possible y-values have been encoded as numbers. Here the species *Iris sestosa* is encoded as (0, 0, 1), *Iris versicolor* is encoded as (0, 1, 0), and the species *Iris virginica* is encoded as (1, 0, 0).

The demo takes the 150-item data set and splits it randomly into a 120-item subset (80%) to be used for training and a 30-item subset (20%) to be used for testing, that is, to be used to estimate the probability of a correct classification on data that has not been seen before. The demo trains a 4-7-2 fully connected neural network using the back-propagation algorithm in conjunction with a technique that is called incremental training.

After training has completed, the accuracy of the resulting model is computed on the training set and on the test set. The model correctly predicts 97.50% of the training items (117 out of 120) and 96.67% of the test items (29 out of 30). Therefore, if presented with data for a new iris flower that was not part of the training or test data, you could estimate that the model would correctly classify the flower with roughly a 0.9667 probability.

Incremental Training

There are two main approaches for training a neural network. As usual, the two approaches have several different names but two of the most common terms are incremental and batch. In high-level pseudo-code, batch training is:

```
loop until done
  for each training item
    compute error and accumulate total error
  end for
  use total error to update weights and bias values
end loop
```

The essence of batch training is that an error metric for the entire training set is computed and then that single error value is used to update all the neural network's weights and biases.

In pseudo-code, incremental training is:

```
loop until done
  for each training item
    compute error for current item
    use item's error to update weights and bias values
  end for
end loop
```

In incremental training, weights and biases are updated for every training item. Based on my conversations, to most people, batch training seems a bit more logical. However, some research evidence suggests that incremental training (also called online training) often gives better results (meaning it produces a model that predicts better) than batch training.

There is a third approach to neural network training, which is a combination of batch and incremental training. The technique is often called mini-batch training. In pseudo-code:

```
loop until done
  loop n times
    compute error term for current item
    accumulate error
  end loop
  use current accumulated error to update weights and bias values
  reset mini accumulated error to 0
end loop
```

The demo program uses incremental training. Notice that in all three training approaches there are two important questions: "How do you determine when training is finished?" and "How do you measure error?" To answer briefly, before the demo code is presented, there is no one best way to determine when training is done. There are two good ways to compute error.

Implementing the Training Demo Program

To create the demo program I launched Visual Studio and created a new C# console application named Training. After the template code loaded into the editor, I removed all using statements except for the single statement referencing the top-level System namespace. The demo program has no significant .NET version dependencies, so any version of Visual Studio should work. In the Solution Explorer window, I renamed file Program.cs to TrainingProgram.cs and Visual Studio automatically renamed the Program class to TrainingProgram.

The overall structure of the demo program is shown in **Listing 5-a**. The Main method in the program class has all the program logic. The program class houses three utility methods: MakeTrainTest, ShowVector, and ShowMatrix. Method ShowMatrix is used by the demo program to display the source data set, which is a matrix in memory, and the training and test matrices. The helper is defined:

```
static void ShowMatrix(double[][] matrix, int numRows, int decimals, bool newLine)
{
  for (int i = 0; i < numRows; ++i)
  {
    Console.Write(i.ToString().PadLeft(3) + ": ");
```

```
        for (int j = 0; j < matrix[i].Length; ++j)
        {
          if (matrix[i][j] >= 0.0) Console.Write(" "); else Console.Write("-");
          Console.Write(Math.Abs(matrix[i][j]).ToString("F" + decimals) + " ");
        }
        Console.WriteLine("");
      }
      if (newLine == true)
        Console.WriteLine("");
}
```

```
using System;
namespace Training
{
  class TrainingProgram
  {
    static void Main(string[] args)
    {
      Console.WriteLine("\nBegin neural network training demo");

      double[][] allData = new double[150][];
      allData[0] = new double[] { 5.1, 3.5, 1.4, 0.2, 0, 0, 1 };
      // Define remaining data here.
      // Create train and test data.

      int numInput = 4;
      int numHidden = 7;
      int numOutput = 3;
      NeuralNetwork nn = new NeuralNetwork(numInput, numHidden, numOutput);

      int maxEpochs = 1000;
      double learnRate = 0.05;
      double momentum = 0.01;
      nn.Train(trainData, maxEpochs, learnRate, momentum);
      Console.WriteLine("Training complete");

      // Display weight and bias values, compute and display model accuracy.
      Console.WriteLine("\nEnd neural network training demo\n");
      Console.ReadLine();
    }

    static void MakeTrainTest(double[][] allData, int seed, out double[][] trainData,
      out double[][] testData) { . . }

    static void ShowVector(double[] vector, int valsPerRow, int decimals,
      bool newLine) { . . }

    static void ShowMatrix(double[][] matrix, int numRows, int decimals,
      bool newLine) { . . }
  }
  public class NeuralNetwork
  {
    private static Random rnd;
    private int numInput;
    private int numHidden;
    private int numOutput;
    // Other fields here.

    public NeuralNetwork(int numInput, int numHidden, int numOutput) { . . }
```

```
    public void SetWeights(double[] weights) { . . }
    public double[] GetWeights() { . . }
    public void Train(double[][] trainData, int maxEprochs, double learnRate,
      double momentum) { . . }
    public double Accuracy(double[][] testData) { . . }

    // class private methods go here.
  }
}
```

Listing 5-a: Overall Demo Program Structure

The numRows parameter to ShowMatrix controls how many rows of the matrix parameter to display, not the total number of rows in the matrix. The method displays row numbers and has a hard-coded column width of 3 for the line numbers. You may want to parameterize whether or not to display row numbers and use the actual number of matrix rows to parameterize the width for line numbers.

The method uses an if-check to determine if the current cell value is positive or zero, and if so, prints a blank space for the implicit "+" sign so that positive values will line up with negative values that have an explicit "-" sign. An alternative is to pass a conditional formatting string argument to the ToString method.

Helper method ShowVector is used by the demo to display the neural network weights and bias values after training has been performed. It is defined:

```
static void ShowVector(double[] vector, int valsPerRow, int decimals, bool newLine)
{
  for (int i = 0; i < vector.Length; ++i)
  {
    if (i % valsPerRow == 0) Console.WriteLine("");
    Console.Write(vector[i].ToString("F" + decimals).PadLeft(decimals + 4) + " ");
  }
  if (newLine == true)
    Console.WriteLine("");
}
```

Creating Training and Test Data

One of the strategies used in neural network training is called hold-out validation. This means to take the available training data, and rather than train the neural network using all the data, remove a portion of the data, typically between 10–30%, to be used to estimate the effectiveness of the trained model. The remaining part of the available data is used for training.

Method MakeTrainTest accepts a matrix of data and returns two matrices. The first return matrix holds a random 80% of the data items and the other matrix is one that holds the other 20% of the data items

In high-level pseudo-code, method MakeTrainTest is:

```
compute number of rows for train matrix := n1
compute number of rows for test matrix := n2
make a copy of the source matrix
scramble the order of the rows of the copy
copy first n1 rows of scrambled-order source copy into train
copy remaining n2 rows of scrambled-order source copy into test
return train and test matrices
```

The implementation of method MakeTrainTest begins:

```
static void MakeTrainTest(double[][] allData, int seed,
  out double[][] trainData, out double[][] testData)
{
  Random rnd = new Random(seed);
```

The method accepts a data matrix to split, and a seed value to initialize the randomization process. The method returns the resulting train and test matrices as out parameters. Although returning multiple results via out parameters is frowned upon in certain circles, in my opinion using this approach is simpler than alternative designs such as using a container class.

Because method MakeTrainTest is called only once in the demo program, it is acceptable to use a Random object with local scope. If the method were called multiple times, the results would be the same unless you passed different seed parameter values on each call.

Next, the method allocates space for the two return matrices like so:

```
int totRows = allData.Length;
int numCols = allData[0].Length;
int trainRows = (int)(totRows * 0.80); // Hard-coded 80-20 split.
int testRows = totRows - trainRows;
trainData = new double[trainRows][];
testData = new double[testRows][];
```

Notice that the method is hard-coded for an 80-20 train-test split. You might want to consider passing the training size as a parameter. This can be tricky because percentages might be in decimal form, such as 0.80, or in percentage form, such as 80.0. Notice that because of possible rounding, it would be risky to compute the number of result rows with code like this:

```
int trainRows = (int)(totRows * 0.80); // risky
int testRows = (int)(totRows * 0.20);
```

Next, method MakeTrainTest makes a reference copy of the source matrix:

```
double[][] copy = new double[allData.Length][];
for (int i = 0; i < copy.Length; ++i)
  copy[i] = allData[i];
```

This code is a bit subtle. Instead of making a copy of the source matrix, it would be perfectly possible to operate directly on the matrix. However this would have the side effect of scrambling the order of the source matrix's rows. The copy of the source matrix is a reference copy. The diagram in **Figure 5-b** shows what a copy of a source matrix with nine rows of data would look like in memory. It would be possible to make a complete copy of the source matrix's values but this would be inefficient and might not even be feasible if the source matrix were very large.

Next the reference copy is randomized:

```
for (int i = 0; i < copy.Length; ++i)
{
  int r = rnd.Next(i, copy.Length);
  double[] tmp = copy[r];
  copy[r] = copy[i];
  copy[i] = tmp;
}
```

The rows of the copy matrix are scrambled using the Fisher-Yates shuffle algorithm which randomly reorders the values in an array. In this case, the values are references to the rows of the copy matrix. The Fisher-Yates shuffle is also quite subtle, but after the code executes, the copy matrix will have the same values as the source but the rows will be in a random order.

Method MakeTrainTest continues by copying rows of the scrambled copy matrix into the trainData result matrix:

```
for (int i = 0; i < trainRows; ++i)
{
  trainData[i] = new double[numCols];
  for (int j = 0; j < numCols; ++j)
  {
    trainData[i][j] = copy[i][j];
  }
}
```

Notice the copy-loop allocates space for the result matrix rows. An alternative would be to perform the allocation in a separate loop.

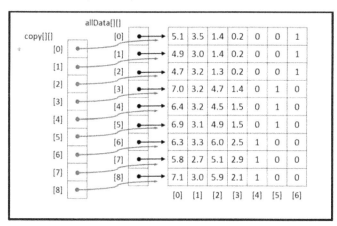

Figure 5-b: Copying a Matrix by Reference

Method MakeTrainTest concludes by copying rows of the scrambled copy matrix into the testData result matrix:

```
  for (int i = 0; i < testRows; ++i) // i points into testData[][]
  {
    testData[i] = new double[numCols];
    for (int j = 0; j < numCols; ++j)
    {
      testData[i][j] = copy[i + trainRows][j]; // be careful
    }
  }
} // MakeTrainTest
```

In this code, variable trainRows will be 120 and testRows will be 30. Row index i points into the testData result matrix and runs from 0 through 29. In the copy assignment, the value i + trainRows points into the source copy matrix and will run from 0 + 120 = 120 through 29 + 120 = 149.

The Main Program Logic

After some preliminary WriteLine statements, the Main method sets up the iris data:

```
static void Main(string[] args)
{
  // Preliminary messages.
  double[][] allData = new double[150][];
  allData[0] = new double[] { 5.1, 3.5, 1.4, 0.2, 0, 0, 1 };
  . . .
  allData[149] = new double[] { 5.9, 3.0, 5.1, 1.8, 1, 0, 0 };
```

For simplicity, the data is placed directly into an array-of-arrays style matrix. Notice the y-data to classify has been pre-encoded as (0, 0, 1), (0, 1, 0), and (1, 0, 0), and that there is an implicit assumption that the y-data occupies the rightmost columns of the matrix. Also, because the x-data values all have roughly the same magnitude, there is no need for data normalization.

In most situations, your data would be in external storage, such as a text file. For example, suppose the demo data were stored in a text file named IrisData.txt with this format:

```
5.1,3.5,1.4,0.2,0,0,1
4.9,3.0,1.4,0.2,0,0,1
. . .
5.9,3.0,5.1,1.8,1,0,0
```

One possible implementation of a method named LoadData to load the data into a matrix is presented in **Listing 5-b**. The method could be called along the lines of:

```
string dataFile = "..\\..\\IrisData.txt";
allData = LoadData(dataFile, 150, 7);
```

In situations where the source data is too large to fit into a matrix in memory, the simplest approach is to stream through the external data source. A complicated alternative is to buffer the streamed data through a matrix.

After loading the data into memory, the Main method displays the first six rows of the data matrix like so:

```
Console.WriteLine("\nFirst 6 rows of the 150-item data set:");
ShowMatrix(allData, 6, 1, true);
```

Next, the demo creates training and test matrices:

```
Console.WriteLine("Creating 80% training and 20% test data matrices");
double[][] trainData = null;
double[][] testData = null;
MakeTrainTest(allData, 72, out trainData, out testData);
```

The rather mysterious looking 72 argument is the seed value passed to the Random object used by method MakeTrainTest. That value was used only because it gave a representative, and pretty, demo output. In most cases you would simply use 0 as the seed value.

```
static double[][] LoadData(string dataFile, int numRows, int numCols)
{
  double[][] result = new double[numRows][];

  FileStream ifs = new FileStream(dataFile, FileMode.Open);
  StreamReader sr = new StreamReader(ifs);
  string line = "";
  string[] tokens = null;
  int i = 0;
  while ((line = sr.ReadLine()) != null)
  {
    tokens = line.Split(',');
    result[i] = new double[numCols];
    for (int j = 0; j < numCols; ++j)
    {
      result[i][j] = double.Parse(tokens[j]);
    }
    ++i;
  }
  sr.Close();
  ifs.Close();
  return result;
}
```

Listing 5-b: Loading Data from a File

The main program logic continues by displaying portions of the newly created training and test data matrices:

```
Console.WriteLine("\nFirst 3 rows of training data:");
ShowMatrix(trainData, 3, 1, true);
Console.WriteLine("First 3 rows of test data:");
ShowMatrix(testData, 3, 1, true);
```

Of course such displays are purely optional when working with neural networks but are often extremely useful during development in order to catch errors early. Total control over your system, including the ability to insert diagnostic display messages anywhere in the system, is a big advantage of writing custom neural network code versus using a packaged system or API library written by someone else.

After creating the training and test matrices, method Main instantiates a neural network:

```
Console.WriteLine("\nCreating a 4-input, 7-hidden, 3-output neural network");
Console.Write("Hard-coded tanh function for input-to-hidden and softmax for ");
Console.WriteLine("hidden-to-output activations");
int numInput = 4;
int numHidden = 7;
int numOutput = 3;
NeuralNetwork nn = new NeuralNetwork(numInput, numHidden, numOutput);
```

The number of input nodes and the number of output nodes are determined by the structure of the source data: four numeric x-values and a y-value with three categorical values. Specifying a good value for the number of hidden nodes is one of the major challenges when working with neural networks. Even though there has been much research done in this area, picking a good value for the number of hidden nodes is mostly a matter of trial and error.

With the data prepared and a neural network instantiated, the Main method performs training like so:

```
int maxEpochs = 1000;
double learnRate = 0.05;
double momentum = 0.01;
Console.WriteLine("Setting maxEpochs = " + maxEpochs + ", learnRate = " +
  learnRate + ", momentum = " + momentum);
Console.WriteLine("Training has hard-coded mean squared " +
  "error < 0.040 stopping condition");
Console.WriteLine("\nBeginning training using incremental back-propagation\n");
nn.Train(trainData, maxEpochs, learnRate, momentum);
Console.WriteLine("Training complete");
```

The maxEpochs variable sets a hard limit on the number of iterations that will be performed in the training code. As you will see shortly, it is not trivial to determine when to stop the main training loop. The learningRate and momentum values control the speed at which the back-propagation converges to a final set of weight and bias values. As it turns out, back-propagation is extremely sensitive to the values used for the learning rate and momentum. Even small changes in these value can have very large effects and can mean the difference between a neural network that predicts well and one that predicts poorly.

For simplicity, the demo neural network has a fourth parameter, an early-exit error threshold value of 0.040 that is hard-coded into method Train. In many situations you would want to parameterize this value along the lines of:

```
int maxEpochs = 1000;
double learnRate = 0.05;
double momentum = 0.01;
double exitError = 0.040;
nn.Train(trainData, maxEpochs, learnRate, momentum, exitError);
```

After training has completed, the demo retrieves and displays the internal weights and bias values that were determined by the training process:

```
double[] weights = nn.GetWeights();
Console.WriteLine("Final neural network weights and bias values:");
ShowVector(weights, 10, 3, true);
```

The Main method concludes by computing and displaying the accuracy of the generated model:

```
  double trainAcc = nn.Accuracy(trainData);
  Console.WriteLine("\nAccuracy on training data = " + trainAcc.ToString("F4"));

  double testAcc = nn.Accuracy(testData);
  Console.WriteLine("\nAccuracy on test data = " + testAcc.ToString("F4"));

  Console.WriteLine("\nEnd neural network training demo\n");
  Console.ReadLine()
} // Main
```

Notice that the accuracy of the neural network on the training data was not used as a condition for stopping training, and is computed only after training has completed. The accuracy of the model on the test data is the more important of the two accuracy metrics. The accuracy of the model on the test data gives you a rough estimate of the accuracy of the model on new data with unknown y-values. A high accuracy on the training data does not necessarily indicate a good model has been generated, but a low accuracy on the test data almost always indicates a poor model.

Training and Error

Method Train is presented in **Listing 5-c**. Although the method is relatively short, it contains several important ideas that must be understood in order for you to be able to modify the code to meet specific problem scenarios.

```
public void Train(double[][] trainData, int maxEpochs, double learnRate, double momentum)
{
  int epoch = 0;
  double[] xValues = new double[numInput]; // Inputs.
  double[] tValues = new double[numOutput]; // Target values.

  int[] sequence = new int[trainData.Length];
  for (int i = 0; i < sequence.Length; ++i)
    sequence[i] = i;

  while (epoch < maxEpochs)
  {
    double mse = MeanSquaredError(trainData);
    if (mse < 0.040) break; // Consider passing value in as parameter.

    Shuffle(sequence); // Visit each training data in random order.
    for (int i = 0; i < trainData.Length; ++i)
    {
      int idx = sequence[i];
      Array.Copy(trainData[idx], xValues, numInput);
```

```
      Array.Copy(trainData[idx], numInput, tValues, 0, numOutput);
      ComputeOutputs(xValues); // Copy xValues in, compute outputs (store them internally).
      UpdateWeights(tValues, learnRate, momentum); // Find better weights and biases.
    } // Each training tuple.
    ++epoch;
  }
}
```

Listing 5-c: Training a Neural Network

The heart of method Train is a while loop that has two exit conditions. The first is a hard limit based on the maxEpochs value. The second exit condition is a small error threshold based on the mean squared error of the current model over the entire training set. Inside the primary outer while-loop is a for-loop that iterates over each item in the training data. The local array named sequence and helper method Shuffle act to make the inner loop visit each training item in a different, random order, each time through the outer loop.

Visiting the training items in a random order is extremely important. Failure to visit training items in a random order is a common mistake and often leads to the training process quickly converging to a poor set of weights and bias values. The key to visiting data items in random order is helper method Shuffle:

```
private static void Shuffle(int[] sequence)
{
  for (int i = 0; i < sequence.Length; ++i)
  {
    int r = rnd.Next(i, sequence.Length);
    int tmp = sequence[r];
    sequence[r] = sequence[i];
    sequence[i] = tmp;
  }
}
```

Method Shuffle accepts an array of array indices and scrambles the order of the indices using the Fisher-Yates algorithm. For example, if a tiny training matrix had just four rows of data and the input parameter array named sequence held values { 0, 1, 2, 3 } then after a call to Shuffle, the values could be { 3, 0, 1, 2 } or any one of the 23 other possible permutations of the ordering.

In the inner for-loop in method Train, index variable i points into the array named sequence and index variable idx points into the rows of the training data matrix. For example, for a four-item training set, if array sequence holds values { 3, 0, 1, 2 } then index variable i takes on values 0, 1, 2, 3; and index variable idx takes on values 3, 0, 1, 2, which is the order in which the training data items would be visited. Notice that the array named sequence needs to be initialized only once, outside the outer while-loop in method Train.

An alternative to the shuffling technique presented here is instead of generating an array of row indices and shuffling the order of the values in that array, actually shuffling the order of the rows of the training data matrix. This would use slightly less memory (no sequence array needed) and have slightly better performance (no assignment to variable idx needed) at the expense of having a side effect (changing the order of the rows of the training data matrix).

The primary training loop in method Train exits when one of two conditions occur: the maximum number of iterations stored in variable maxEpochs is reached, or when the mean squared error drops below a hard-coded 0.040 value. Understanding and modifying the training-loop exit is one of the most important features of working with neural networks.

At first thought, it would seem that a reasonable strategy would be to simply train a neural network for as many iterations as possible. This approach often leads to over-fitting, a situation where the resulting model's weight and bias values fit the training data very well (often nearly perfectly) but when presented with new data, the model predicts very poorly.

The technique used by the demo is to use a moderate number for the hard-stop loop exit combined with the mean squared error (MSE). MSE is perhaps best explained by example. Suppose a mini training set of iris flower data consisted of just two training items:

```
5.0, 3.0, 1.5, 0.5, 0, 0, 1
6.0, 3.5, 1.7, 0.4, 0, 1, 0
```

Now suppose that for a given set of weights and bias values, the computed outputs for the two data items are (0.2, 0.1, 0.7) and (0.3, 0.6, 0.1) respectively. The squared error for the first training data item is $(0 - 0.2)^2 + (0 - 0.1)^2 + (1 - 0.7)^2 = 0.04 + 0.01 + 0.09 = 0.14$. The squared error for the second training data item is $(0 - 0.3)^2 + (1 - 0.6)^2 + (0 - 0.1)^2 = 0.09 + 0.16 + 0.01 = 0.26$. The total squared error of the mini training data set is $0.14 + 0.26 = 0.40$. So, the mean (average) squared error, MSE, for the two items is $0.40 / 2 = 0.20$.

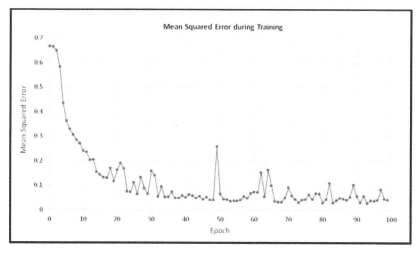

Figure 5-c: Mean Squared Error

A common approach to terminating training is to exit when the MSE drops below some threshold. This is the technique used by the demo program. Although reasonable, the approach does have a weakness. Typically, during neural network training, the MSE does not decrease in a completely smooth, monotonic manner. Instead, the MSE jumps around a bit. For example, the graph in **Figure 5-c** shows how MSE changes over time for the demo program. The data was generated simply by inserting this statement inside the outer while-loop in method Train:

```
Console.WriteLine(epoch + " " + mse.ToString("F4"));
```

Suppose the early-exit MSE threshold value were set to 0.15 (an artificially large value). If you examine the graph between epochs 10 and 30 closely, you can see that the MSE drops below 0.15 at epoch 15. However, the MSE jumps above 0.15 at epoch 20. The point is that using a single MSE exit threshold value is simple and usually effective, but runs the risk of stopping training too early.

One interesting approach to the loop-exit issue is to divide all available data into three sets rather than just training and test sets. The third set is called the validation set. For example, using a 60-20-20 split for the 150-item Fisher's Iris data, 90 items (60% of 150) would be in the training set, 30 items (20% of 150) would be in the test set, and the remaining 30 items would be in the validation set.

You would train the neural network using the training data, but inside the main training loop you would compute the MSE on the validation set. Over time the MSE on the validation set would drop but at some point, when over-fitting begins to occur, the MSE on the validation set would begin to increase. You would identify at what epoch the MSE on the validation set began to steadily increase (either programmatically or visually by graphing MSE) and then use the weights and bias values at that epoch for the final neural network model. And then you would compute the accuracy of the model on the unused test data set to get an estimate of the model's accuracy for new data.

Helper method MeanSquaredError is presented in **Listing 5-d**. Notice that in both method Train and in method MeanSquaredError, arrays xValues and tValues are used to store the values of the current input values and target values, and that the values are copied in by value rather than reference from the training data matrix. This is simple and effective but somewhat inefficient. An alternative is to make copies by reference.

Also notice that in all methods of the demo program, there is an implicit assumption that the encoded y-values occupy the last numOutput columns of the training matrix. When working with neural networks, there is no standard way to store data internally. The encoded y-values can be stored in the last columns of a training matrix as in the demo program, in the first columns, or the x-values and y-values can be stored in separate matrices. How to store training data is an important design decision and one that affects the code in many of the methods used during training.

```
private double MeanSquaredError(double[][] trainData)
{
  // Average squared error per training item.
  double sumSquaredError = 0.0;
  double[] xValues = new double[numInput]; // First numInput values in trainData.
  double[] tValues = new double[numOutput]; // Last numOutput values.

  // Walk through each training case. Looks like (6.9 3.2 5.7 2.3) (0 0 1).
```

```
    for (int i = 0; i < trainData.Length; ++i)
    {
      Array.Copy(trainData[i], xValues, numInput); // Get input x-values.
      Array.Copy(trainData[i], numInput, tValues, 0, numOutput); // Get target values.
      double[] yValues = this.ComputeOutputs(xValues); // Compute output using current
 weights.
      for (int j = 0; j < numOutput; ++j)
      {
        double err = tValues[j] - yValues[j];
        sumSquaredError += err * err;
      }
    }

    return sumSquaredError / trainData.Length;
}
```

Listing 5-d: Computing Mean Squared Error

The MSE value is an average error per training item and so an error-exit threshold value does not depend on the number of training items there are. However, if you refer back to how MSE is computed, you can see that MSE does depend to some extent on the number of possible classes there are in the y-data. Therefore, an alternative to using a fixed MSE threshold is to use a value that is based on the number of output values, for example 0.005 * numOutput.

Method Train computes and checks the MSE value on every iteration through the training loop. Computing MSE is a relatively expensive operation, so an alternative is to compute MSE only every 10 or 100 or 1,000 iterations along the lines of:

```
if (epoch % 100 == 0)
{
  double mse = MeanSquaredError(trainData);
  if (mse < 0.040) break;
}
```

Computing Accuracy

The code for public class method Accuracy is presented in **Listing 5-e**. How method Accuracy works is best explained using a concrete example. Suppose the computed output values and the desired target values for three training items are:

```
0.2   0.1   0.7    0   0   1
0.1   0.6   0.3    0   1   0
0.4   0.5   0.1    1   0   0
```

For the first data item, the three computed output values of 0.2, 0.1, and 0.7 can be loosely interpreted to mean the probabilities of the three possible categorical y-values. The demo program uses a technique called winner-takes-all. The idea is to find the highest probability, in this case 0.7, and then check the associated desired target value to see if it is 1 (a correct prediction) or 0 (an incorrect prediction). Because the third target output is a 1, the first data item was correctly predicted.

```
public double Accuracy(double[][] testData)
{
  // Percentage correct using winner-takes all.
  int numCorrect = 0;
  int numWrong = 0;
  double[] xValues = new double[numInput]; // Inputs.
  double[] tValues = new double[numOutput]; // Targets.
  double[] yValues; // Computed Y.

  for (int i = 0; i < testData.Length; ++i)
  {
    Array.Copy(testData[i], xValues, numInput); // Get x-values and t-values.
    Array.Copy(testData[i], numInput, tValues, 0, numOutput);
    yValues = this.ComputeOutputs(xValues);
    int maxIndex = MaxIndex(yValues); // Which cell in yValues has the largest value?

    if (tValues[maxIndex] == 1.0)
      ++numCorrect;
    else
      ++numWrong;
  }
  return (numCorrect * 1.0) / (numCorrect + numWrong);
}
```

Listing 5-e: Computing Model Accuracy

For the second data item, the largest computed output is 0.6 which is in the second position, which corresponds to a target value of 1, so the second data item is also a correct prediction.

For the third data item, the largest computed output is 0.5. The associated target value is 0, so the third data item is an incorrect prediction.

Method Accuracy uses a helper method MaxIndex to find the location of the largest computed y-value. The helper is defined:

```
private static int MaxIndex(double[] vector)
{
  int bigIndex = 0;
  double biggestVal = vector[0];
  for (int i = 0; i < vector.Length; ++i)
  {
    if (vector[i] > biggestVal)
    {
      biggestVal = vector[i];
      bigIndex = i;
    }
  }
  return bigIndex;
}
```

Notice that method MaxIndex does not take into account the possibility that there may be two or more computed y-values that have equal magnitude. In practice this is usually not a problem, but for a neural network that is part of some critical system you would want to handle this possibility at the expense of slightly slower performance.

Method Accuracy also has two implementation choices that you may want to modify depending on your particular problem scenario. First, the method does a check for exact equality between value tValues[maxIndex] and the constant value 1.0. Because many type double values are just extremely close approximations to their true values, a more robust approach would be to check if tVlaues[maxIndex] is within some very small value (typically called epsilon) of 1.0. For example:

```
if (Math.Abs(tValues[maxIndex] - 1.0) < 0.000000001)
  ++numCorrect;
```

In practice, checking for the exact equality of an array value and the constant 1.0 is usually not a problem. The second implementation issue in method Accuracy is that the computation of the return value does not perform a division by zero check. This could only happen if the quantity numCorrect + numWrong were equal to 0. The ability to deliberately take intelligent shortcuts like this to improve performance and reduce code complexity is a big advantage of writing custom neural network code for your own use.

At first thought, it might seem that instead of using some error metric such as MSE to determine when to stop training, it would be preferable to use the accuracy of the neural network on the training data using its current weight and bias values. After all, in the end, prediction accuracy, not error, is the most important characteristic of a neural network. However, using accuracy to determine when to stop training is not as effective as using error. For example, suppose a neural network, Model A, has computed and target output values:

```
0.1  0.2  0.7   0  0  1
0.1  0.8  0.1   0  1  0
0.3  0.3  0.4   1  0  0
```

Model A correctly predicts the first two data items but misses the third and so has a classification accuracy of 2/3 = 0.6667. The MSE for Model A is (0.14 + 0.06 + 0.74) / 3 = 0.3133.

Now consider a Model B with computed and target output values of:

```
0.3  0.3  0.4   0  0  1
0.3  0.4  0.3   0  1  0
0.1  0.1  0.8   1  0  0
```

Model B also predicts the first two data items correctly and so has a classification accuracy of 0.6667. But Model B is clearly worse than Model A. Model B just barely gets the first two items correct and misses badly on the third. The MSE for Model B is (0.54 + 0.54 + 1.46) / 3 = 0.8467 which is more than twice as large as the MSE for Model A. In short, classification accuracy is too coarse of a metric to use during training.

Cross Entropy Error

There is an important alternative to mean squared error called mean cross entropy error. There is some strong, but not entirely conclusive, research evidence to suggest that for many classification problems, using mean cross entropy error generates better models than using mean squared error. Exactly what cross entropy error is, is best explained by example. Suppose that for some neural network there are just two training items with three computed output values and three associated desired target output values:

```
0.1  0.2  0.7    0  0  1
0.3  0.6  0.1    0  1  0
```

The cross entropy error for the first data item is computed as:

$-((\ln(0.1) * 0) + (\ln(0.2) * 0) + (\ln(0.7) * 1)) = -(0 + 0 + (-0.36)) = 0.36$

The cross entropy error for the second data item is:

$-((\ln(0.3) * 0) + (\ln(0.6) * 1) + (\ln(0.1) * 0)) = -(0 + (-0.51) + 0) = 0.51$

Here ln is the natural logarithm function. The mean (average) cross entropy error is (0.36 + 0.51) / 2 = 0.435. Notice the odd-looking multiplications by 0. This is a consequence of the mathematical definition of cross entropy error and the fact that for neural classification problems all target values except one will have value 0. One possible implementation of a mean cross entropy error function is presented in **Listing 5-f**.

Using mean cross entropy error is very deep mathematically but simple in practice. First, mean cross entropy error can be used as a training-loop exit condition in exactly the same way as mean squared error. The second way to use mean cross entropy error is during the back-propagation routine during training. In the demo program, method Train calls method ComputeOutputs to perform the feed-forward part of training and calls method UpdateWeights to modify all neural network weights and bias values using the back-propagation algorithm.

```
private double MeanCrossEntropyError(double[][] trainData)
{
  double sumError = 0.0;
  double[] xValues = new double[numInput]; // First numInput values in trainData.
  double[] tValues = new double[numOutput]; // Last numOutput values.

  for (int i = 0; i < trainData.Length; ++i) // Training data: (6.9 3.2 5.7 2.3) (0 0 1).
  {
    Array.Copy(trainData[i], xValues, numInput); // Get xValues.
    Array.Copy(trainData[i], numInput, tValues, 0, numOutput); // Get target values.
    double[] yValues = this.ComputeOutputs(xValues); // Compute output using current
weights.
    for (int j = 0; j < numOutput; ++j)
    {
      sumError += Math.Log(yValues[j]) * tValues[j]; // CE error for one training data.
    }
  }
  return -1.0 * sumError / trainData.Length;
}
```

Listing 5-f: Mean Cross Entropy Error

As it turns out, the back-propagation algorithm is making an implicit assumption about what error metric is being used behind the scenes. This assumption is needed to compute a calculus derivative which in turn is implemented in code. Put another way, if you examine the code for the back-propagation algorithm inside method UpdateWeights you will not see an explicit error term being computed. The error term used is actually mean squared error but it is computed implicitly and has an effect when the gradient values for the hidden layer and output layer nodes are computed.

Therefore, if you want to use mean cross entropy error for neural network training, you need to know what the implicit effect on back-propagation in method UpdateWeights is. Inside method UpdateWeights, the implicit mean squared error code occurs in two places. The first is the computation of the output node gradient values. The computation of output gradients with an assumption of the standard MSE is:

```
for (int i = 0; i < numOutput; ++i)
{
  double derivative = (1 - outputs[i]) * outputs[i]; // Softmax activation.
  oGrads[i] = derivative * (tValues[i] - outputs[i]);
}
```

The computation of output gradients with an assumption of cross entropy error is rather amazing:

```
for (int i = 0; i < numOutput; ++i)
{
  oGrads[i] = tValues[i] - outputs[i]; // Assumes softmax.
}
```

In essence, the derivative term drops out altogether. Actually, the derivative is still computed when using cross entropy error but several terms cancel each other out leaving the remarkably simple result that the output gradient is just the target value minus the computed output value.

This result is one of the most surprising in neural networks. Because of the simplicity of the gradient term when using cross entropy error, it is sometimes said that cross entropy is the natural error term to use with neural network classification problems.

The second place where the implied error term emerges is in the computation of the hidden node gradient values. The hidden node gradient code which assumes MSE is:

```
for (int i = 0; i < numHidden; ++i)
{
  double derivative = (1 - hOutputs[i]) * (1 + hOutputs[i]); // tanh
  double sum = 0.0;
  for (int j = 0; j < numOutput; ++j)
  {
    double x = oGrads[j] * hoWeights[i][j];
    sum += x;
  }
  hGrads[i] = derivative * sum;
}
```

To modify this code so that it implicitly uses mean cross entropy error you would likely guess that the derivative term vanishes here too. However, again, somewhat surprisingly, this time the code does not change at all. You can find the elegant but complex mathematical derivations of the computation of back-propagation gradient values for both MSE and cross entropy error in many places on the Internet.

Binary Classification Problems

The iris data classification problem has three possible categorical y-values. Problems that have only two possible categorical y-values are very common. You can image predicting a person's sex (male or female) based on x-data like height, occupation, left or right hand dominance, and so on. Or consider predicting a person's credit worthiness (approve loan, reject loan) based on things like credit score, current debt, annual income, and so on.

Classification problems where the y-value to predict can be one of two values are called binary classification problems. Problems where there are three or more categorical y-values to predict are sometimes called multinomial classification problems to distinguish them from binary classification problems.

Dealing with a binary classification problem can in principle be done using the exact same techniques as those used for multinomial classification problems. For example, suppose the iris data file contained only data for two species, *Iris setosa* and *Iris versicolor* along the lines of:

```
5.1, 3.5, 1.4, 0.2, Iris-setosa
4.9, 3.0, 1.4, 0.2, Iris-setosa
. . .
5.7, 2.8, 4.1, 1.3, Iris-versicolor
```

You could encode the data like so:

```
5.1, 3.5, 1.4, 0.2, 0, 1
4.9, 3.0, 1.4, 0.2, 0, 1
. . .
5.7, 2.8, 4.1, 1.3, 1, 0
```

Here, *Iris setosa* is encoded as (0, 1) and *Iris versicolor* is encoded as (1, 0). Your neural network would have four input nodes and two output nodes. The network would use softmax activation on the output nodes and generate two computed outputs that sum to 1.0. For example, for the first data item in the previous example with target values of (0, 1), the computed output values might be (0.2, 0.8). In short, you would use the exact same technique for a binary problem as when there are three or more possible y-values.

However, binary classification problems can be encoded using a single value rather than two values. This is a consequence of the fact that, if you have two values that must sum to 1.0, and you know just one of the two values, you automatically know what the other value must be.

So, the previous data could be encoded as:

```
5.1, 3.5, 1.4, 0.2, 0
4.9, 3.0, 1.4, 0.2, 0
. . .
5.7, 2.8, 4.1, 1.3, 1
```

where *Iris setosa* is encoded as a 0 and *Iris versicolor* is encoded as a 1. If you encode using this 0-1 way, you must make two changes to the approach used by the demo program for multinomial classification.

First, when computing neural network output values, using softmax activation for the output layer nodes will not work because softmax assumes there are two or more nodes and coerces them to sum to 1.0. If you encode a binary classification problem using a 0-1 approach then you should use the logistic sigmoid function for output layer activation. For example, suppose you define the logistic sigmoid as:

```
public double LogSigmoid(double x)
{
  if (x < -45.0)
    return 0.0;
  else if (x > 45.0)
    return 1.0;
  else
    return 1.0 / (1.0 + Math.Exp(-x));
}
```

Then in method ComputeOutputs, the following lines of code:

```
double[] softOut = Softmax(oSums); // All outputs at once.
Array.Copy(softOut, outputs, softOut.Length);
```

would be replaced by this:

```
for (int i = 0; i < numOutput; ++i) // Single output node.
  outputs[i] = LogSigmoid(oSums[i]);
```

Because the logistic sigmoid function and the softmax function both have the same calculus derivatives, you do not need to make any changes to the back-propagation algorithm. And the hyperbolic tangent function remains a good choice for hidden layer activation for 0-1 encoded binary classification problems.

When using 0-1 encoding for a binary classification problem, the second change occurs in computing classification accuracy. Instead of finding the index of the largest computed output value and checking to see if the associated target value is 1.0, you just examine the single computed value and check to see if it is less than or equal to 0.5 (corresponding to a target y-value of 0) or greater than 0.5 (corresponding to a target y-value of 1).

For example, inside class method Accuracy, the code for softmax output is:

```
int maxIndex = MaxIndex(yValues); // Which cell in yValues has the largest value?
if (tValues[maxIndex] == 1.0)
  ++numCorrect;
```

```
else
  ++numWrong;
```

Those two statements would be replaced with:

```
if (yValues[0] <= 0.5 && tValues[0] == 0.0)
  ++numCorrect;
else if (yValues[0] > 0.5 && tValues[0] == 1.0)
  ++numCorrect;
else
  ++numWrong;
```

Notice that with 0-1 encoding both the tValues target outputs array and the yValues computed outputs array will have a length of just one cell and so are referenced by tValues[0] and yValues[0]. You could refactor all occurrences of the tValues and yValues arrays to simple variables of type double, but this would require a lot of work for no significant gain.

To recap, when working with a binary classification problem you can encode the first y-value as (0, 1), the second y-value as (1, 0), and use the exact same code as in the demo which works with multinomial classification. Or you can encode the first y-value as 0, the second y-value as 1, and make two changes to the demo neural network (in method ComputeOutputs and method Accuracy).

Among my colleagues, the vast majority prefer to use 0-1 encoding for binary classification problems. Their argument is that the alternative of using (0, 1) and (1, 0) encoding creates additional weights and biases that must be found during training. I prefer using (0, 1) and (1, 0) encoding for binary classification problems. My argument is that I only need a single code base for both binary and multinomial problems.

Complete Demo Program Source Code

```
using System;
namespace Training
{
  class TrainingProgram
  {
    static void Main(string[] args)
    {
      Console.WriteLine("\nBegin neural network training demo");
      Console.WriteLine("\nData is the famous Iris flower set.");
      Console.WriteLine("Predict species from sepal length, width, petal length, width");
      Console.WriteLine("Iris setosa = 0 0 1, versicolor = 0 1 0, virginica = 1 0 0 \n");

      Console.WriteLine("Raw data resembles:");
      Console.WriteLine(" 5.1, 3.5, 1.4, 0.2, Iris setosa");
      Console.WriteLine(" 7.0, 3.2, 4.7, 1.4, Iris versicolor");
      Console.WriteLine(" 6.3, 3.3, 6.0, 2.5, Iris virginica");
      Console.WriteLine(" ......\n");

      double[][] allData = new double[150][];
      allData[0] = new double[] { 5.1, 3.5, 1.4, 0.2, 0, 0, 1 };
      allData[1] = new double[] { 4.9, 3.0, 1.4, 0.2, 0, 0, 1 }; // Iris setosa = 0 0 1
      allData[2] = new double[] { 4.7, 3.2, 1.3, 0.2, 0, 0, 1 }; // Iris versicolor = 0 1 0
```

```java
allData[3] = new double[] { 4.6, 3.1, 1.5, 0.2, 0, 0, 1 }; // Iris virginica = 1 0 0
allData[4] = new double[] { 5.0, 3.6, 1.4, 0.2, 0, 0, 1 };
allData[5] = new double[] { 5.4, 3.9, 1.7, 0.4, 0, 0, 1 };
allData[6] = new double[] { 4.6, 3.4, 1.4, 0.3, 0, 0, 1 };
allData[7] = new double[] { 5.0, 3.4, 1.5, 0.2, 0, 0, 1 };
allData[8] = new double[] { 4.4, 2.9, 1.4, 0.2, 0, 0, 1 };
allData[9] = new double[] { 4.9, 3.1, 1.5, 0.1, 0, 0, 1 };

allData[10] = new double[] { 5.4, 3.7, 1.5, 0.2, 0, 0, 1 };
allData[11] = new double[] { 4.8, 3.4, 1.6, 0.2, 0, 0, 1 };
allData[12] = new double[] { 4.8, 3.0, 1.4, 0.1, 0, 0, 1 };
allData[13] = new double[] { 4.3, 3.0, 1.1, 0.1, 0, 0, 1 };
allData[14] = new double[] { 5.8, 4.0, 1.2, 0.2, 0, 0, 1 };
allData[15] = new double[] { 5.7, 4.4, 1.5, 0.4, 0, 0, 1 };
allData[16] = new double[] { 5.4, 3.9, 1.3, 0.4, 0, 0, 1 };
allData[17] = new double[] { 5.1, 3.5, 1.4, 0.3, 0, 0, 1 };
allData[18] = new double[] { 5.7, 3.8, 1.7, 0.3, 0, 0, 1 };
allData[19] = new double[] { 5.1, 3.8, 1.5, 0.3, 0, 0, 1 };

allData[20] = new double[] { 5.4, 3.4, 1.7, 0.2, 0, 0, 1 };
allData[21] = new double[] { 5.1, 3.7, 1.5, 0.4, 0, 0, 1 };
allData[22] = new double[] { 4.6, 3.6, 1.0, 0.2, 0, 0, 1 };
allData[23] = new double[] { 5.1, 3.3, 1.7, 0.5, 0, 0, 1 };
allData[24] = new double[] { 4.8, 3.4, 1.9, 0.2, 0, 0, 1 };
allData[25] = new double[] { 5.0, 3.0, 1.6, 0.2, 0, 0, 1 };
allData[26] = new double[] { 5.0, 3.4, 1.6, 0.4, 0, 0, 1 };
allData[27] = new double[] { 5.2, 3.5, 1.5, 0.2, 0, 0, 1 };
allData[28] = new double[] { 5.2, 3.4, 1.4, 0.2, 0, 0, 1 };
allData[29] = new double[] { 4.7, 3.2, 1.6, 0.2, 0, 0, 1 };

allData[30] = new double[] { 4.8, 3.1, 1.6, 0.2, 0, 0, 1 };
allData[31] = new double[] { 5.4, 3.4, 1.5, 0.4, 0, 0, 1 };
allData[32] = new double[] { 5.2, 4.1, 1.5, 0.1, 0, 0, 1 };
allData[33] = new double[] { 5.5, 4.2, 1.4, 0.2, 0, 0, 1 };
allData[34] = new double[] { 4.9, 3.1, 1.5, 0.1, 0, 0, 1 };
allData[35] = new double[] { 5.0, 3.2, 1.2, 0.2, 0, 0, 1 };
allData[36] = new double[] { 5.5, 3.5, 1.3, 0.2, 0, 0, 1 };
allData[37] = new double[] { 4.9, 3.1, 1.5, 0.1, 0, 0, 1 };
allData[38] = new double[] { 4.4, 3.0, 1.3, 0.2, 0, 0, 1 };
allData[39] = new double[] { 5.1, 3.4, 1.5, 0.2, 0, 0, 1 };

allData[40] = new double[] { 5.0, 3.5, 1.3, 0.3, 0, 0, 1 };
allData[41] = new double[] { 4.5, 2.3, 1.3, 0.3, 0, 0, 1 };
allData[42] = new double[] { 4.4, 3.2, 1.3, 0.2, 0, 0, 1 };
allData[43] = new double[] { 5.0, 3.5, 1.6, 0.6, 0, 0, 1 };
allData[44] = new double[] { 5.1, 3.8, 1.9, 0.4, 0, 0, 1 };
allData[45] = new double[] { 4.8, 3.0, 1.4, 0.3, 0, 0, 1 };
allData[46] = new double[] { 5.1, 3.8, 1.6, 0.2, 0, 0, 1 };
allData[47] = new double[] { 4.6, 3.2, 1.4, 0.2, 0, 0, 1 };
allData[48] = new double[] { 5.3, 3.7, 1.5, 0.2, 0, 0, 1 };
allData[49] = new double[] { 5.0, 3.3, 1.4, 0.2, 0, 0, 1 };

allData[50] = new double[] { 7.0, 3.2, 4.7, 1.4, 0, 1, 0 };
allData[51] = new double[] { 6.4, 3.2, 4.5, 1.5, 0, 1, 0 };
allData[52] = new double[] { 6.9, 3.1, 4.9, 1.5, 0, 1, 0 };
allData[53] = new double[] { 5.5, 2.3, 4.0, 1.3, 0, 1, 0 };
allData[54] = new double[] { 6.5, 2.8, 4.6, 1.5, 0, 1, 0 };
allData[55] = new double[] { 5.7, 2.8, 4.5, 1.3, 0, 1, 0 };
allData[56] = new double[] { 6.3, 3.3, 4.7, 1.6, 0, 1, 0 };
allData[57] = new double[] { 4.9, 2.4, 3.3, 1.0, 0, 1, 0 };
allData[58] = new double[] { 6.6, 2.9, 4.6, 1.3, 0, 1, 0 };
```

```
allData[59] = new double[] { 5.2, 2.7, 3.9, 1.4, 0, 1, 0 };

allData[60] = new double[] { 5.0, 2.0, 3.5, 1.0, 0, 1, 0 };
allData[61] = new double[] { 5.9, 3.0, 4.2, 1.5, 0, 1, 0 };
allData[62] = new double[] { 6.0, 2.2, 4.0, 1.0, 0, 1, 0 };
allData[63] = new double[] { 6.1, 2.9, 4.7, 1.4, 0, 1, 0 };
allData[64] = new double[] { 5.6, 2.9, 3.6, 1.3, 0, 1, 0 };
allData[65] = new double[] { 6.7, 3.1, 4.4, 1.4, 0, 1, 0 };
allData[66] = new double[] { 5.6, 3.0, 4.5, 1.5, 0, 1, 0 };
allData[67] = new double[] { 5.8, 2.7, 4.1, 1.0, 0, 1, 0 };
allData[68] = new double[] { 6.2, 2.2, 4.5, 1.5, 0, 1, 0 };
allData[69] = new double[] { 5.6, 2.5, 3.9, 1.1, 0, 1, 0 };

allData[70] = new double[] { 5.9, 3.2, 4.8, 1.8, 0, 1, 0 };
allData[71] = new double[] { 6.1, 2.8, 4.0, 1.3, 0, 1, 0 };
allData[72] = new double[] { 6.3, 2.5, 4.9, 1.5, 0, 1, 0 };
allData[73] = new double[] { 6.1, 2.8, 4.7, 1.2, 0, 1, 0 };
allData[74] = new double[] { 6.4, 2.9, 4.3, 1.3, 0, 1, 0 };
allData[75] = new double[] { 6.6, 3.0, 4.4, 1.4, 0, 1, 0 };
allData[76] = new double[] { 6.8, 2.8, 4.8, 1.4, 0, 1, 0 };
allData[77] = new double[] { 6.7, 3.0, 5.0, 1.7, 0, 1, 0 };
allData[78] = new double[] { 6.0, 2.9, 4.5, 1.5, 0, 1, 0 };
allData[79] = new double[] { 5.7, 2.6, 3.5, 1.0, 0, 1, 0 };

allData[80] = new double[] { 5.5, 2.4, 3.8, 1.1, 0, 1, 0 };
allData[81] = new double[] { 5.5, 2.4, 3.7, 1.0, 0, 1, 0 };
allData[82] = new double[] { 5.8, 2.7, 3.9, 1.2, 0, 1, 0 };
allData[83] = new double[] { 6.0, 2.7, 5.1, 1.6, 0, 1, 0 };
allData[84] = new double[] { 5.4, 3.0, 4.5, 1.5, 0, 1, 0 };
allData[85] = new double[] { 6.0, 3.4, 4.5, 1.6, 0, 1, 0 };
allData[86] = new double[] { 6.7, 3.1, 4.7, 1.5, 0, 1, 0 };
allData[87] = new double[] { 6.3, 2.3, 4.4, 1.3, 0, 1, 0 };
allData[88] = new double[] { 5.6, 3.0, 4.1, 1.3, 0, 1, 0 };
allData[89] = new double[] { 5.5, 2.5, 4.0, 1.3, 0, 1, 0 };

allData[90] = new double[] { 5.5, 2.6, 4.4, 1.2, 0, 1, 0 };
allData[91] = new double[] { 6.1, 3.0, 4.6, 1.4, 0, 1, 0 };
allData[92] = new double[] { 5.8, 2.6, 4.0, 1.2, 0, 1, 0 };
allData[93] = new double[] { 5.0, 2.3, 3.3, 1.0, 0, 1, 0 };
allData[94] = new double[] { 5.6, 2.7, 4.2, 1.3, 0, 1, 0 };
allData[95] = new double[] { 5.7, 3.0, 4.2, 1.2, 0, 1, 0 };
allData[96] = new double[] { 5.7, 2.9, 4.2, 1.3, 0, 1, 0 };
allData[97] = new double[] { 6.2, 2.9, 4.3, 1.3, 0, 1, 0 };
allData[98] = new double[] { 5.1, 2.5, 3.0, 1.1, 0, 1, 0 };
allData[99] = new double[] { 5.7, 2.8, 4.1, 1.3, 0, 1, 0 };

allData[100] = new double[] { 6.3, 3.3, 6.0, 2.5, 1, 0, 0 };
allData[101] = new double[] { 5.8, 2.7, 5.1, 1.9, 1, 0, 0 };
allData[102] = new double[] { 7.1, 3.0, 5.9, 2.1, 1, 0, 0 };
allData[103] = new double[] { 6.3, 2.9, 5.6, 1.8, 1, 0, 0 };
allData[104] = new double[] { 6.5, 3.0, 5.8, 2.2, 1, 0, 0 };
allData[105] = new double[] { 7.6, 3.0, 6.6, 2.1, 1, 0, 0 };
allData[106] = new double[] { 4.9, 2.5, 4.5, 1.7, 1, 0, 0 };
allData[107] = new double[] { 7.3, 2.9, 6.3, 1.8, 1, 0, 0 };
allData[108] = new double[] { 6.7, 2.5, 5.8, 1.8, 1, 0, 0 };
allData[109] = new double[] { 7.2, 3.6, 6.1, 2.5, 1, 0, 0 };

allData[110] = new double[] { 6.5, 3.2, 5.1, 2.0, 1, 0, 0 };
allData[111] = new double[] { 6.4, 2.7, 5.3, 1.9, 1, 0, 0 };
allData[112] = new double[] { 6.8, 3.0, 5.5, 2.1, 1, 0, 0 };
allData[113] = new double[] { 5.7, 2.5, 5.0, 2.0, 1, 0, 0 };
```

```
allData[114] = new double[] { 5.8, 2.8, 5.1, 2.4, 1, 0, 0 };
allData[115] = new double[] { 6.4, 3.2, 5.3, 2.3, 1, 0, 0 };
allData[116] = new double[] { 6.5, 3.0, 5.5, 1.8, 1, 0, 0 };
allData[117] = new double[] { 7.7, 3.8, 6.7, 2.2, 1, 0, 0 };
allData[118] = new double[] { 7.7, 2.6, 6.9, 2.3, 1, 0, 0 };
allData[119] = new double[] { 6.0, 2.2, 5.0, 1.5, 1, 0, 0 };

allData[120] = new double[] { 6.9, 3.2, 5.7, 2.3, 1, 0, 0 };
allData[121] = new double[] { 5.6, 2.8, 4.9, 2.0, 1, 0, 0 };
allData[122] = new double[] { 7.7, 2.8, 6.7, 2.0, 1, 0, 0 };
allData[123] = new double[] { 6.3, 2.7, 4.9, 1.8, 1, 0, 0 };
allData[124] = new double[] { 6.7, 3.3, 5.7, 2.1, 1, 0, 0 };
allData[125] = new double[] { 7.2, 3.2, 6.0, 1.8, 1, 0, 0 };
allData[126] = new double[] { 6.2, 2.8, 4.8, 1.8, 1, 0, 0 };
allData[127] = new double[] { 6.1, 3.0, 4.9, 1.8, 1, 0, 0 };
allData[128] = new double[] { 6.4, 2.8, 5.6, 2.1, 1, 0, 0 };
allData[129] = new double[] { 7.2, 3.0, 5.8, 1.6, 1, 0, 0 };

allData[130] = new double[] { 7.4, 2.8, 6.1, 1.9, 1, 0, 0 };
allData[131] = new double[] { 7.9, 3.8, 6.4, 2.0, 1, 0, 0 };
allData[132] = new double[] { 6.4, 2.8, 5.6, 2.2, 1, 0, 0 };
allData[133] = new double[] { 6.3, 2.8, 5.1, 1.5, 1, 0, 0 };
allData[134] = new double[] { 6.1, 2.6, 5.6, 1.4, 1, 0, 0 };
allData[135] = new double[] { 7.7, 3.0, 6.1, 2.3, 1, 0, 0 };
allData[136] = new double[] { 6.3, 3.4, 5.6, 2.4, 1, 0, 0 };
allData[137] = new double[] { 6.4, 3.1, 5.5, 1.8, 1, 0, 0 };
allData[138] = new double[] { 6.0, 3.0, 4.8, 1.8, 1, 0, 0 };
allData[139] = new double[] { 6.9, 3.1, 5.4, 2.1, 1, 0, 0 };

allData[140] = new double[] { 6.7, 3.1, 5.6, 2.4, 1, 0, 0 };
allData[141] = new double[] { 6.9, 3.1, 5.1, 2.3, 1, 0, 0 };
allData[142] = new double[] { 5.8, 2.7, 5.1, 1.9, 1, 0, 0 };
allData[143] = new double[] { 6.8, 3.2, 5.9, 2.3, 1, 0, 0 };
allData[144] = new double[] { 6.7, 3.3, 5.7, 2.5, 1, 0, 0 };
allData[145] = new double[] { 6.7, 3.0, 5.2, 2.3, 1, 0, 0 };
allData[146] = new double[] { 6.3, 2.5, 5.0, 1.9, 1, 0, 0 };
allData[147] = new double[] { 6.5, 3.0, 5.2, 2.0, 1, 0, 0 };
allData[148] = new double[] { 6.2, 3.4, 5.4, 2.3, 1, 0, 0 };
allData[149] = new double[] { 5.9, 3.0, 5.1, 1.8, 1, 0, 0 };

//string dataFile = "..\\..\\IrisData.txt";
//allData = LoadData(dataFile, 150, 7);

Console.WriteLine("\nFirst 6 rows of the 150-item data set:");
ShowMatrix(allData, 6, 1, true);

Console.WriteLine("Creating 80% training and 20% test data matrices");
double[][] trainData = null;
double[][] testData = null;
MakeTrainTest(allData, 72, out trainData, out testData); // seed = 72 gives a pretty
demo.

Console.WriteLine("\nFirst 3 rows of training data:");
ShowMatrix(trainData, 3, 1, true);
Console.WriteLine("First 3 rows of test data:");
ShowMatrix(testData, 3, 1, true);

Console.WriteLine("\nCreating a 4-input, 7-hidden, 3-output neural network");
Console.Write("Hard-coded tanh function for input-to-hidden and softmax for ");
Console.WriteLine("hidden-to-output activations");
int numInput = 4;
```

```
      int numHidden = 7;
      int numOutput = 3;
      NeuralNetwork nn = new NeuralNetwork(numInput, numHidden, numOutput);

      int maxEpochs = 1000;
      double learnRate = 0.05;
      double momentum = 0.01;

      Console.WriteLine("Setting maxEpochs = " + maxEpochs + ", learnRate = " +
        learnRate + ", momentum = " + momentum);
      Console.WriteLine("Training has hard-coded mean squared " +
        "error < 0.040 stopping condition");

      Console.WriteLine("\nBeginning training using incremental back-propagation\n");
      nn.Train(trainData, maxEpochs, learnRate, momentum);
      Console.WriteLine("Training complete");

      double[] weights = nn.GetWeights();
      Console.WriteLine("Final neural network weights and bias values:");
      ShowVector(weights, 10, 3, true);

      double trainAcc = nn.Accuracy(trainData);
      Console.WriteLine("\nAccuracy on training data = " + trainAcc.ToString("F4"));

      double testAcc = nn.Accuracy(testData);
      Console.WriteLine("\nAccuracy on test data = " + testAcc.ToString("F4"));

      Console.WriteLine("\nEnd neural network training demo\n");
      Console.ReadLine();

    } // Main

    static void MakeTrainTest(double[][] allData, int seed, out double[][] trainData,
      out double[][] testData)
    {
      // Split allData into 80% trainData and 20% testData.
      Random rnd = new Random(seed);
      int totRows = allData.Length;
      int numCols = allData[0].Length;

      int trainRows = (int)(totRows * 0.80); // Hard-coded 80-20 split.
      int testRows = totRows - trainRows;

      trainData = new double[trainRows][];
      testData = new double[testRows][];

      double[][] copy = new double[allData.Length][]; // Make a reference copy.
      for (int i = 0; i < copy.Length; ++i)
        copy[i] = allData[i];

      // Scramble row order of copy.
      for (int i = 0; i < copy.Length; ++i)
      {
        int r = rnd.Next(i, copy.Length);
        double[] tmp = copy[r];
        copy[r] = copy[i];
        copy[i] = tmp;
      }

      // Copy first trainRows from copy[][] to trainData[][].
      for (int i = 0; i < trainRows; ++i)
```

```
    {
      trainData[i] = new double[numCols];
      for (int j = 0; j < numCols; ++j)
      {
        trainData[i][j] = copy[i][j];
      }
    }

    // Copy testRows rows of allData[] into testData[][].
    for (int i = 0; i < testRows; ++i) // i points into testData[][].
    {
      testData[i] = new double[numCols];
      for (int j = 0; j < numCols; ++j)
      {
        testData[i][j] = copy[i + trainRows][j];
      }
    }
} // MakeTrainTest

static void ShowVector(double[] vector, int valsPerRow, int decimals, bool newLine)
{
  for (int i = 0; i < vector.Length; ++i)
  {
    if (i % valsPerRow == 0) Console.WriteLine("");
    Console.Write(vector[i].ToString("F" + decimals).PadLeft(decimals + 4) + " ");
  }
  if (newLine == true) Console.WriteLine("");
}

static void ShowMatrix(double[][] matrix, int numRows, int decimals, bool newLine)
{
  for (int i = 0; i < numRows; ++i)
  {
    Console.Write(i.ToString().PadLeft(3) + ": ");
    for (int j = 0; j < matrix[i].Length; ++j)
    {
      if (matrix[i][j] >= 0.0) Console.Write(" "); else Console.Write("-");
      Console.Write(Math.Abs(matrix[i][j]).ToString("F" + decimals) + " ");
    }
    Console.WriteLine("");
  }
  if (newLine == true)
    Console.WriteLine("");
}

//static double[][] LoadData(string dataFile, int numRows, int numCols)
//{
//  double[][] result = new double[numRows][];

//  FileStream ifs = new FileStream(dataFile, FileMode.Open);
//  StreamReader sr = new StreamReader(ifs);
//  string line = "";
//  string[] tokens = null;
//  int i = 0;
//  while ((line = sr.ReadLine()) != null)
//  {
//    tokens = line.Split(',');
//    result[i] = new double[numCols];
//    for (int j = 0; j < numCols; ++j)
//    {
//      result[i][j] = double.Parse(tokens[j]);
```

```
//    }
//    ++i;
//  }
//  sr.Close();
//  ifs.Close();
//  return result;
//}

} // class Program


public class NeuralNetwork
{
  private static Random rnd;

  private int numInput;
  private int numHidden;
  private int numOutput;

  private double[] inputs;

  private double[][] ihWeights; // input-hidden
  private double[] hBiases;
  private double[] hOutputs;

  private double[][] hoWeights; // hidden-output
  private double[] oBiases;

  private double[] outputs;

  // Back-propagation specific arrays.
  private double[] oGrads; // Output gradients.
  private double[] hGrads;

  // Back-propagation momentum-specific arrays.
  private double[][] ihPrevWeightsDelta;
  private double[] hPrevBiasesDelta;
  private double[][] hoPrevWeightsDelta;
  private double[] oPrevBiasesDelta;

  public NeuralNetwork(int numInput, int numHidden, int numOutput)
  {
    rnd = new Random(0); // For InitializeWeights() and Shuffle().

    this.numInput = numInput;
    this.numHidden = numHidden;
    this.numOutput = numOutput;

    this.inputs = new double[numInput];

    this.ihWeights = MakeMatrix(numInput, numHidden);
    this.hBiases = new double[numHidden];
    this.hOutputs = new double[numHidden];

    this.hoWeights = MakeMatrix(numHidden, numOutput);
    this.oBiases = new double[numOutput];

    this.outputs = new double[numOutput];

    this.InitializeWeights();
```

```
      // Back-propagation related arrays below.
      this.hGrads = new double[numHidden];
      this.oGrads = new double[numOutput];

      this.ihPrevWeightsDelta = MakeMatrix(numInput, numHidden);
      this.hPrevBiasesDelta = new double[numHidden];
      this.hoPrevWeightsDelta = MakeMatrix(numHidden, numOutput);
      this.oPrevBiasesDelta = new double[numOutput];
    } // ctor

    private static double[][] MakeMatrix(int rows, int cols) // Helper for ctor.
    {
      double[][] result = new double[rows][];
      for (int r = 0; r < result.Length; ++r)
        result[r] = new double[cols];
      return result;
    }

    // --------------------------------------------------------------------------
---

    public void SetWeights(double[] weights)
    {
      // Copy weights and biases in weights[] array to i-h weights, i-h biases,
      // h-o weights, h-o biases.
      int numWeights = (numInput * numHidden) + (numHidden * numOutput) +
        numHidden + numOutput;
      if (weights.Length != numWeights)
        throw new Exception("Bad weights array length: ");

      int k = 0; // Points into weights param.

      for (int i = 0; i < numInput; ++i)
        for (int j = 0; j < numHidden; ++j)
          ihWeights[i][j] = weights[k++];
      for (int i = 0; i < numHidden; ++i)
        hBiases[i] = weights[k++];
      for (int i = 0; i < numHidden; ++i)
        for (int j = 0; j < numOutput; ++j)
          hoWeights[i][j] = weights[k++];
      for (int i = 0; i < numOutput; ++i)
        oBiases[i] = weights[k++];
    }

    private void InitializeWeights()
    {
      // Initialize weights and biases to small random values.
      int numWeights = (numInput * numHidden) + (numHidden * numOutput) +
        numHidden + numOutput;
      double[] initialWeights = new double[numWeights];
      double lo = -0.01;
      double hi = 0.01;
      for (int i = 0; i < initialWeights.Length; ++i)
        initialWeights[i] = (hi - lo) * rnd.NextDouble() + lo;
      this.SetWeights(initialWeights);
    }

    public double[] GetWeights()
    {
      // Returns the current set of weights, presumably after training.
      int numWeights = (numInput * numHidden) + (numHidden * numOutput) +
```

```
      numHidden + numOutput;
    double[] result = new double[numWeights];
    int k = 0;
    for (int i = 0; i < ihWeights.Length; ++i)
      for (int j = 0; j < ihWeights[0].Length; ++j)
        result[k++] = ihWeights[i][j];
    for (int i = 0; i < hBiases.Length; ++i)
      result[k++] = hBiases[i];
    for (int i = 0; i < hoWeights.Length; ++i)
      for (int j = 0; j < hoWeights[0].Length; ++j)
        result[k++] = hoWeights[i][j];
    for (int i = 0; i < oBiases.Length; ++i)
      result[k++] = oBiases[i];
    return result;
  }

  // -------------------------------------------------------------------------------------

  private double[] ComputeOutputs(double[] xValues)
  {
    if (xValues.Length != numInput)
      throw new Exception("Bad xValues array length");

    double[] hSums = new double[numHidden]; // Hidden nodes sums scratch array.
    double[] oSums = new double[numOutput]; // Output nodes sums.

    for (int i = 0; i < xValues.Length; ++i) // Copy x-values to inputs.
      this.inputs[i] = xValues[i];

    for (int j = 0; j < numHidden; ++j)  // Compute i-h sum of weights * inputs.
      for (int i = 0; i < numInput; ++i)
        hSums[j] += this.inputs[i] * this.ihWeights[i][j]; // note +=

    for (int i = 0; i < numHidden; ++i)  // Add biases to input-to-hidden sums.
      hSums[i] += this.hBiases[i];

    for (int i = 0; i < numHidden; ++i)  // Apply activation.
      this.hOutputs[i] = HyperTan(hSums[i]); // Hard-coded.

    for (int j = 0; j < numOutput; ++j)  // Compute h-o sum of weights * hOutputs.
      for (int i = 0; i < numHidden; ++i)
        oSums[j] += hOutputs[i] * hoWeights[i][j];

    for (int i = 0; i < numOutput; ++i)  // Add biases to input-to-hidden sums.
      oSums[i] += oBiases[i];

    double[] softOut = Softmax(oSums); // All outputs at once for efficiency.
    Array.Copy(softOut, outputs, softOut.Length);

    double[] retResult = new double[numOutput];
    Array.Copy(this.outputs, retResult, retResult.Length);
    return retResult;
  } // ComputeOutputs

  private static double HyperTan(double x)
  {
    if (x < -20.0)
      return -1.0; // Approximation is correct to 30 decimals.
    else if (x > 20.0)
      return 1.0;
    else return
```

```
        Math.Tanh(x);
    }

    private static double[] Softmax(double[] oSums)
    {
      // Does all output nodes at once so scale doesn't have to be re-computed each time.
      double max = oSums[0];        // Determine max output sum.
      for (int i = 0; i < oSums.Length; ++i)
        if (oSums[i] > max) max = oSums[i];

      // Determine scaling factor -- sum of exp(each val - max).
      double scale = 0.0;
      for (int i = 0; i < oSums.Length; ++i)
        scale += Math.Exp(oSums[i] - max);

      double[] result = new double[oSums.Length];
      for (int i = 0; i < oSums.Length; ++i)
        result[i] = Math.Exp(oSums[i] - max) / scale;

      return result; // Now scaled so that xi sum to 1.0.
    }

    // ----------------------------------------------------------------------------


    private void UpdateWeights(double[] tValues, double learnRate, double momentum)
    {
      // Update the weights and biases using back-propagation.
      // Assumes that SetWeights and ComputeOutputs have been called
      // and matrices have values (other than 0.0).
      if (tValues.Length != numOutput)
        throw new Exception("target values not same Length as output in UpdateWeights");

      // 1. Compute output gradients.
      for (int i = 0; i < numOutput; ++i)
      {
        // Derivative for softmax = (1 - y) * y (same as log-sigmoid).
        double derivative = (1 - outputs[i]) * outputs[i];
        // 'Mean squared error version' includes (1-y)(y) derivative.
        oGrads[i] = derivative * (tValues[i] - outputs[i]);
      }

      // 2. Compute hidden gradients.
      for (int i = 0; i < numHidden; ++i)
      {
        // Derivative of tanh = (1 - y) * (1 + y).
        double derivative = (1 - hOutputs[i]) * (1 + hOutputs[i]);
        double sum = 0.0;
        for (int j = 0; j < numOutput; ++j) // Each hidden delta is the sum of numOutput
terms.
        {
          double x = oGrads[j] * hoWeights[i][j];
          sum += x;
        }
        hGrads[i] = derivative * sum;
      }

      // 3a. Update hidden weights (gradients must be computed right-to-left but weights
      // can be updated in any order).
      for (int i = 0; i < numInput; ++i) // 0..2 (3)
      {
```

```
      for (int j = 0; j < numHidden; ++j) // 0..3 (4)
      {
        double delta = learnRate * hGrads[j] * inputs[i]; // Compute the new delta.
        ihWeights[i][j] += delta; // Update -- note '+' instead of '-'.
        // Now add momentum using previous delta.
        ihWeights[i][j] += momentum * ihPrevWeightsDelta[i][j];
        ihPrevWeightsDelta[i][j] = delta; // Don't forget to save the delta for momentum .
      }
    }

    // 3b. Update hidden biases.
    for (int i = 0; i < numHidden; ++i)
    {
      double delta = learnRate * hGrads[i]; // 1.0 is constant input for bias.
      hBiases[i] += delta;
      hBiases[i] += momentum * hPrevBiasesDelta[i]; // Momentum.
      hPrevBiasesDelta[i] = delta; // Don't forget to save the delta.
    }

    // 4. Update hidden-output weights.
    for (int i = 0; i < numHidden; ++i)
    {
      for (int j = 0; j < numOutput; ++j)
      {
        double delta = learnRate * oGrads[j] * hOutputs[i];
        hoWeights[i][j] += delta;
        hoWeights[i][j] += momentum * hoPrevWeightsDelta[i][j]; // Momentum.
        hoPrevWeightsDelta[i][j] = delta; // Save.
      }
    }

    // 4b. Update output biases.
    for (int i = 0; i < numOutput; ++i)
    {
      double delta = learnRate * oGrads[i] * 1.0;
      oBiases[i] += delta;
      oBiases[i] += momentum * oPrevBiasesDelta[i]; // Momentum.
      oPrevBiasesDelta[i] = delta; // save
    }
  } // UpdateWeights

  // --------------------------------------------------------------------------------

  public void Train(double[][] trainData, int maxEpochs, double learnRate, double
momentum)
  {
    // Train a back-propagation style NN classifier using learning rate and momentum.
    int epoch = 0;
    double[] xValues = new double[numInput]; // Inputs.
    double[] tValues = new double[numOutput]; // Target values.

    int[] sequence = new int[trainData.Length];
    for (int i = 0; i < sequence.Length; ++i)
      sequence[i] = i;

    while (epoch < maxEpochs)
    {
      double mse = MeanSquaredError(trainData);
      if (mse < 0.040) break; // Consider passing value in as parameter.

      Shuffle(sequence); // Visit each training data in random order.
```

```
        for (int i = 0; i < trainData.Length; ++i)
        {
          int idx = sequence[i];
          Array.Copy(trainData[idx], xValues, numInput);
          Array.Copy(trainData[idx], numInput, tValues, 0, numOutput);
          ComputeOutputs(xValues); // Copy xValues in, compute outputs (store them
internally).
          UpdateWeights(tValues, learnRate, momentum); // Find better weights.
        } // Each training item.
        ++epoch;
      }
    } // Train

    private static void Shuffle(int[] sequence)
    {
      for (int i = 0; i < sequence.Length; ++i)
      {
        int r = rnd.Next(i, sequence.Length);
        int tmp = sequence[r];
        sequence[r] = sequence[i];
        sequence[i] = tmp;
      }
    }

    private double MeanSquaredError(double[][] trainData) // Training stopping condition.
    {
      // Average squared error per training item.
      double sumSquaredError = 0.0;
      double[] xValues = new double[numInput]; // First numInput values in trainData.
      double[] tValues = new double[numOutput]; // Last numOutput values.

      // Walk through each training case. Looks like (6.9 3.2 5.7 2.3) (0 0 1).
      for (int i = 0; i < trainData.Length; ++i)
      {
        Array.Copy(trainData[i], xValues, numInput);
        Array.Copy(trainData[i], numInput, tValues, 0, numOutput); // Get target values.
        double[] yValues = this.ComputeOutputs(xValues); // Outputs using current weights.
        for (int j = 0; j < numOutput; ++j)
        {
          double err = tValues[j] - yValues[j];
          sumSquaredError += err * err;
        }
      }

      return sumSquaredError / trainData.Length;
    }

    // ----------------------------------------------------------------------------

    public double Accuracy(double[][] testData)
    {
      // Percentage correct using winner-takes all.
      int numCorrect = 0;
      int numWrong = 0;
      double[] xValues = new double[numInput]; // Inputs.
      double[] tValues = new double[numOutput]; // Targets.
      double[] yValues; // Computed Y.

      for (int i = 0; i < testData.Length; ++i)
      {
        Array.Copy(testData[i], xValues, numInput); // Get x-values.
```

```
      Array.Copy(testData[i], numInput, tValues, 0, numOutput); // Get t-values.
      yValues = this.ComputeOutputs(xValues);
      int maxIndex = MaxIndex(yValues); // Which cell in yValues has the largest value?

      if (tValues[maxIndex] == 1.0) // ugly
        ++numCorrect;
      else
        ++numWrong;
    }
    return (numCorrect * 1.0) / (numCorrect + numWrong); // No check for divide by zero.
  }

  private static int MaxIndex(double[] vector) // Helper for Accuracy().
  {
    // Index of largest value.
    int bigIndex = 0;
    double biggestVal = vector[0];
    for (int i = 0; i < vector.Length; ++i)
    {
      if (vector[i] > biggestVal)
      {
        biggestVal = vector[i];
        bigIndex = i;
      }
    }
    return bigIndex;
  }
} // class NeuralNetwork
} // ns
```

www.ingramcontent.com/pod-product-compliance
Lightning Source LLC
Chambersburg PA
CBHW071254050326
40690CB00011B/2388